Microsoft® PowerPoint® Notes

for use with

Financial Accounting

Fourth Edition

Robert Libby
Cornell University – Ithaca

Patricia A. Libby
Ithaca College

Daniel G. Short
Miami University – Oxford

Prepared by

Jon A. Booker
Charles W. Caldwell
Richard S. Rand
All of Tennessee Technological University

Susan C. Galbreath
David Lipscomb University

 Irwin

Boston   Burr Ridge, IL   Dubuque, IA   Madison, WI   New York   San Francisco   St. Louis
Bangkok   Bogotá   Caracas   Kuala Lumpur   Lisbon   London   Madrid   Mexico City
Milan   Montreal   New Delhi   Santiago   Seoul   Singapore   Sydney   Taipei   Toronto

Microsoft® PowerPoint® Notes for use with
FINANCIAL ACCOUNTING
Robert Libby, Patricia A. Libby, Daniel G. Short

Published by McGraw-Hill/Irwin, an imprint of The McGraw-Hill Companies, Inc., 1221 Avenue of the Americas, New York, NY 10020. Copyright © 1996, 1998, 2001, 2004 by The McGraw-Hill Companies, Inc. All rights reserved.

1 2 3 4 5 6 7 8 9 0 CUS/CUS 0 9 8 7 6 5 4 3 2

ISBN 0-07-247365-7

www.mhhe.com

Welcome to

Microsoft® PowerPoint® Notes

Your life just got easier! This booklet includes *Microsoft® PowerPoint® Notes* to accompany your textbook. This booklet was designed as a classroom supplement to accompany *Microsoft® PowerPoint® Slides*. More importantly, *Microsoft® PowerPoint® Notes* were developed for you, the student.

Somewhere in your educational experience, you have undoubtedly encountered a common dilemma facing many students; the feeling of helplessness that comes from trying to write down everything your instructor says and, at the same time, actually paying attention to what is being taught. *Microsoft® PowerPoint® Notes* addresses this problem by providing pre-prepared lecture outlines to accompany the *Microsoft® PowerPoint® Slides* your instructor will be using in class. Rather than spending time copying material that is already in the book, you will be able to focus on the most important aspects of what your instructor is actually saying. You will still be expected to take notes, but the nature of those notes will change.

Each page in *Microsoft® PowerPoint® Notes* includes reproductions of some of the actual projected screens that you will be seeing in class. The *Microsoft® PowerPoint® Notes* booklet includes the information for many of the examples that your instructor will be presenting.

It is your responsibility to attend class regularly and to be prepared for class. However, used properly, *Microsoft® PowerPoint® Notes* will help you to achieve your goals for the course. Good luck and good accounting!

CONTENTS

FINANCIAL ACCOUNTING

Robert Libby
Patricia A. Libby
Daniel G. Short

Chapter 1

Financial Statements and Business Decisions

Understanding the Business

Owner-Managers	Founders of the business who also function as managers are called Owner-Mangers.
Creditors	Creditors lend money for a specific period of time and gain by charging interest on the money they lend.
Investors	Investors buy ownership in the company in the form of stock.

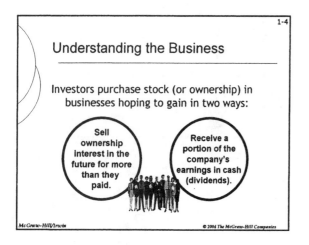

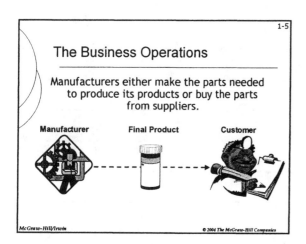

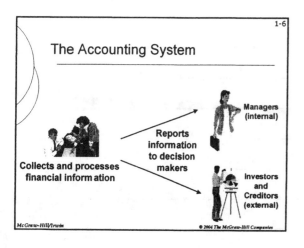

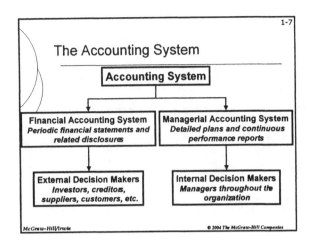

The Accounting System

Accounting System

Financial Accounting System
Periodic financial statements and related disclosures

Managerial Accounting System
Detailed plans and continuous performance reports

External Decision Makers
Investors, creditors, suppliers, customers, etc.

Internal Decision Makers
Managers throughout the organization

McGraw-Hill/Irwin   © 2004 The McGraw-Hill Companies

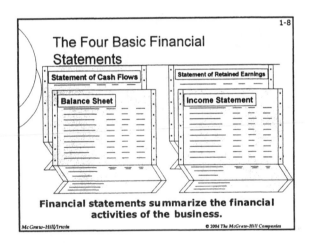

The Four Basic Financial Statements

Statement of Cash Flows

Statement of Retained Earnings

Balance Sheet

Income Statement

Financial statements summarize the financial activities of the business.

McGraw-Hill/Irwin   © 2004 The McGraw-Hill Companies

The Four Basic Financial Statements

Companies can prepare financial statements at the end of the year, quarter or month.

2003

Financial statements prepared at the end of the year are called annual reports.

McGraw-Hill/Irwin   © 2004 The McGraw-Hill Companies

Let's look at MAXIDRIVE CORP.'s financial statements.

1. Name of entity	MAXIDRIVE CORP.		
2. Title of statement	Balance Sheet		
3. Specific date	At December 31, 2003		
4. Unit of measure	(in thousands of dollars)		
	Assets		
	Cash		$ 4,895
	Accounts receivable		5,714
	Inventories		8,517
	Plant and equipment		7,154
	Land		981
	Total assets		$ 27,261
	Liabilities and Stockholders' Equity		
	Liabilities		
	Accounts payable	$ 7,156	
	Notes payable	9,000	
	Total liabilities		$ 16,156
	Stockholders' Equity		
	Contributed capital	$ 2,000	
	Retained earnings	9,105	
	Total stockholders' equity		11,105
	Total liabilities and stockholders' equity		$ 27,261

The Balance Sheet reports the financial position of an entity at a particular point in time.

McGraw-Hill/Irwin

The Balance Sheet

Basic Accounting Equation

Assets = Liabilities + Stockholders' Equity

McGraw-Hill/Irwin © 2004 The McGraw-Hill Companies

Slide 1

MAXIDRIVE CORP.
Balance Sheet
At December 31, 2003
(in thousands of dollars)

Assets are economic resources owned by the business as a result of past transactions.

Assets	
Cash	$ 4,895
Accounts receivable	5,714
Inventories	8,517
Plant and equipment	7,154
Land	981
Total assets	$ 27,261

Assets are listed by their ease of conversion into cash.

Cash	Amount of cash in the company's bank accounts.
Accounts receivable	Amounts owed by customers from prior sales.
Inventories	Parts and completed but unsold products.
Plant and equipment	Factories and production machinery.
Land	Land on which factories are built.

McGraw-Hill/Irwin

Slide 2

MAXIDRIVE CORP.
Balance Sheet
At December 31, 2003
(in thousands of dollars)

Liabilities are debts or obligations of the business that result from past transactions.

Assets	
Cash	$ 4,895
Accounts receivable	5,714
Inventories	8,517
Plant and equipment	7,154
Land	981
Total assets	$ 27,261
Liabilities and Stockholders' Equity	
Liabilities	
Accounts payable	$ 7,156
Notes payable	9,000
Total liabilities	$ 16,156

Accounts payable	Amounts owed to suppliers for prior purchases.
Notes payable	Amounts owed on written debt contracts.

	$ 2,000	
	9,105	
		11,105
Total liabilities and stockholders' equity		$ 27,261

McGraw-Hill/Irwin

Slide 3

MAXIDRIVE CORP.
Balance Sheet
At December 31, 2003
(in thousands of dollars)

Equity is the amount of financing provided by owners of the business and earnings.

Assets	
Cash	$ 4,895
Accounts receivable	5,714
Inventories	8,517
Plant and equipment	7,154
Land	981
Total assets	$ 27,261
Liabilities and Stockholders' Equity	

Contributed capital	Amounts invested in the business by stockholders.
Retained earnings	Past earnings not distributed to stockholders.

	$ 7,156	
	9,000	
		$ 16,156
Stockholders' Equity		
Contributed capital	$ 2,000	
Retained earnings	9,105	
Total stockholders' equity		11,105
Total liabilities and stockholders' equity		$ 27,261

McGraw-Hill/Irwin

MAXIDRIVE CORP.
Balance Sheet
At December 31, 2003
(in thousands of dollars)

Assets		
Cash		$ 4,895
Accounts receivable		5,714
Inventories		8,517
Plant and equipment		7,154
Land		981
Total assets		$ 27,261
Liabilities and Stockholders' Equity		
Liabilities		
Accounts payable	7,156	
Notes payable	9,000	
		$ 16,156
Stockholders' Equity		
Contributed capital	2,000	
Retained earnings	9,105	
Total stockholders' equity		11,105
Total liabilities and stockholders' equity		$ 27,261

Use $ on the first item in a group and on the group total.

Assets = Liabilities + Stockholders' Equity

McGraw-Hill/Irwin

1-17

MAXIDRIVE CORP.
Income Statement
For the Year Ended December 31, 2003
(in thousands of dollars)

Revenues

1. Name of entity
2. Title of statement
3. Specific date (Unlike the balance sheet, this statement covers a specified period of time.)
4. Unit of measure

Interest expense	450	
Total expenses		33,036
Pretax income		$ 4,400
Income tax expense		1,100
Net income		$ 3,300

McGraw-Hill/Irwin

1-18

The Income Statement reports the revenues less expenses of the accounting period.

Revenues		
Sales revenue		$ 37,436
Expenses		
Cost of goods sold	$ 26,980	
Selling, general and administrative	3,624	
Research and development	1,982	
Interest expense	450	
Total expenses		33,036
Pretax income		$ 4,400
Income tax expense		1,100
Net income		$ 3,300

McGraw-Hill/Irwin

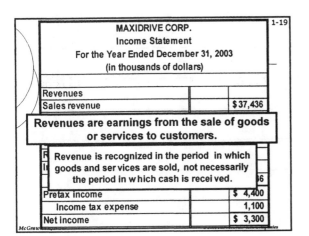

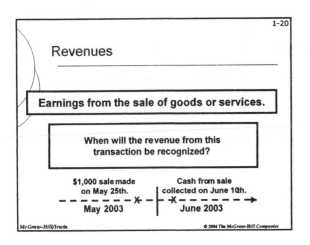

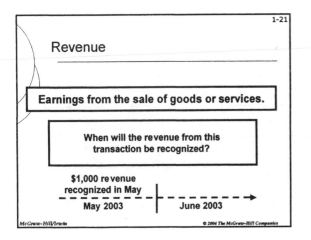

Expenses are the dollar amount of resources used up by the entity to earn revenues during a period.

An expense is recognized in the period in which goods and services are used, not necessarily the period in which cash is paid.

Expenses		
Cost of goods sold	$26,980	
Selling, general and administrative	3,624	
Research and development	1,982	
Interest expense	450	
Total expenses		33,036
Pretax income		$ 4,400
Income tax expense		1,100
Net income		$ 3,300

McGraw-Hill/Irwin

MAXIDRIVE CORP.
Income Statement
For the Year Ended December 31, 2003
(in thousands of dollars)

Cost of goods sold	The cost to produce products sold this period.
Selling, general and administrative	Operating expenses not directly related to production.
Research and development	Expenses incurred to develop new products.
Interest expense	The cost of using borrowed funds.
Income tax expense	Income taxes on current period's pretax income.

McGraw-Hill/Irwin

Expenses

The dollar amount of resources used up by the entity to earn revenues during a period.

When will the expense for this transaction be recognized?

May 11 paid $75 cash for newspaper ad.

Ad appears on June 8th.

May 2003   June 2003

McGraw-Hill/Irwin   © 2004 The McGraw-Hill Companies

Expenses

The dollar amount of resources used up by the entity to earn re venues during a period.

When will the expense for this transaction be recognized?

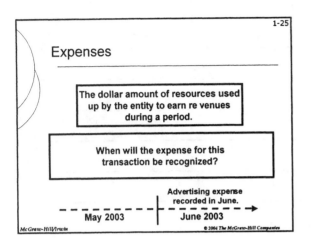

Advertising expense recorded in June.

May 2003 — June 2003

MAXIDRIVE CORP. Income Statement For the Year Ended December 31, 2003 (in thousands of dollars)		
Revenues		
Sales revenue		$ 37,436
Expenses		
Cost of goods sold	$ 26,980	
Selling, general and administrative	3,624	
Research and development	1,982	
Interest expense	450	
Total expenses		33,036
Pretax income		$ 4,400

If expenses exceed revenues, we report net loss.

MAXIDRIVE CORP. Statement of Retained Earnings For the Year Ended December 31, 2003 (in thousands of dollars)	
Retained earnings, January 1, 2003	$ 6,805

1. Name of entity
2. Title of statem ent
3. Specific date (Like the incom e statement, this statement co vers a specified per iod of time.)
4. Unit of m easure

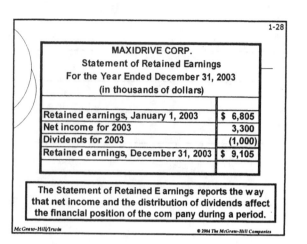

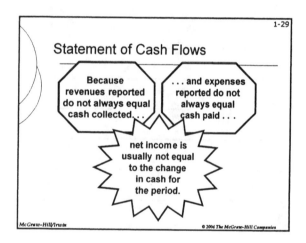

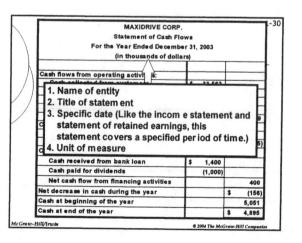

Slide 1-31

The Statement of Cash Flows reports the inflows and outflows of cash during the period in the categories of operating, investing, and financing.

Cash flows from operating activities:		
Cash collected from customers	$ 33,563	
Cash paid to suppliers and employees	(30,854)	
Cash paid for interest	(450)	
Cash paid for taxes	(1,190)	
Net cash flow from operating activities		$ 1,069
Cash flow from investing activities:		
Cash paid to purchase equipment	$ (1,625)	
Net cash flow from investing activities		(1,625)
Cash flow from financing activities:		
Cash received from bank loan	$ 1,400	
Cash paid for dividends	(1,000)	
Net cash flow from financing activities		400
Net decrease in cash during the year		$ (156)
Cash at beginning of the year		5,051
Cash at end of the year		$ 4,895

McGraw-Hill/Irwin   © 2004 The McGraw-Hill Companies

Slide 1-32

MAXIDRIVE CORP.
Statement of Cash Flows
For the Year Ended December 31, 2003
(in thousands of dollars)

Cash flows from operating activities:		
Cash collected from customers	$ 33,563	
Cash paid to suppliers and employees	(30,854)	
Cash paid for interest	(450)	
Cash paid for taxes	(1,190)	

Cash flows directly related to earning income are shown in the operating section.

Cash paid for dividends	(1,000)	
Net cash flow from financing activities		400
Net decrease in cash during the year		$ (156)
Cash at beginning of the year		5,051

McGraw-Hill/Irwin   © 2004 The McGraw-Hill Companies

Slide 1-33

MAXIDRIVE CORP.
Statement of Cash Flows
For the Year Ended December 31, 2003

Cash flows related to the acquisition or sale of productive assets are shown in the investing section.

Cash flow from investing activities:		
Cash paid to purchase equipment	$ (1,625)	
Net cash flow from investing activities		(1,625)
Cash flow from financing activities:		
Cash received from bank loan	$ 1,400	
Cash paid for dividends	(1,000)	
Net cash flow from financing activities		400
Net decrease in cash during the year		$ (156)
Cash at beginning of the year		5,051
Cash at end of the year		$ 4,895

McGraw-Hill/Irwin   © 2004 The McGraw-Hill Companies

MAXIDRIVE CORP.
Statement of Cash Flows
For the Year Ended December 31, 2003
(in thousands of dollars)

1-34

Cash flows from operating activities:		
Cash collected from customers	$ 33,563	
Cash paid to suppliers and employees	(30,854)	

Cash flows from or to investors or creditors are shown in the financing section.

Cash flow from financing activities:		
Cash received from bank loan	$ 1,400	
Cash paid for dividends	(1,000)	
Net cash flow from financing activities		400
Net decrease in cash during the year		$ (156)
Cash at beginning of the year		5,051
Cash at end of the year		$ 4,895

McGraw-Hill/Irwin © 2004 The McGraw-Hill Companies

MAXIDRIVE CORP.
Statement of Cash Flows
For the Year Ended December 31, 2003
(in thousands of dollars)

1-35

Cash flows from operating activities:		
Cash collected from customers	$ 33,563	
Cash paid to suppliers and employees	(30,854)	
Cash paid for interest	(450)	
Cash paid for taxes	(1,190)	
Net cash flow from operating activities		$ 1,069
Cash flow from investing activities:		

The statement ends with a reconciliation of Cash.

Net decrease in cash during the year		$ (156)
Cash at beginning of the year		5,051
Cash at end of the year		$ 4,895

McGraw-Hill/Irwin © 2004 The McGraw-Hill Companies

1-36

Relationship Among the Financial Statements

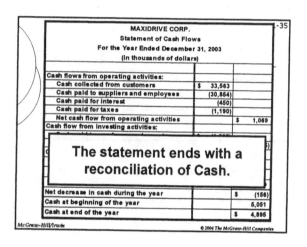

Net income from the income statement increases ending retained earnings on the statement of retained earnings.

MAXIDRIVE CORP.
Statement of Retained Earnings
For the Year Ended December 31, 2003
(in thousands of dollars)

Retained earnings, January 1, 2003	$ 6,805
Net income for 2003	3,300
Dividends for 2003	(1,000)
Retained earnings, December 31, 2003	$ 9,105

McGraw-Hill/Irwin © 2004 The McGraw-Hill Companies

Slide 1-37

Relationship Among the Financial Statements

MAXIDRIVE CORP.
Balance Sheet
At December 31, 2003
(in thousands of dollars)

Assets	
Cash	$ 4,895
Accounts receivable	5,714
Inventories	8,517
Plant and equipment	7,154
Land	981
Total assets	$ 27,261
Liabilities and Stockholders' Equity	
Liabilities	
Accounts payable	$ 7,156
Notes payable	9,000
Total liabilities	$ 16,156
Stockholders' Equity	
Contributed capital	$ 2,000
Retained earnings	9,105
Total stockholders' equity	11,105
Total liabilities and stockholders' equity	$ 27,261

Ending retained earnings from the statement of retained earnings is one of the components of stockholders' equity on the balance sheet.

MAXIDRIVE CORP.
Statement of Retained Earnings
For the Year Ended December 31, 2003
(in thousands of dollars)

Retained earnings, January 1, 2003	$ 6,805
Net income for 2003	3,300
Dividends for 2003	(1,000)
Retained earnings, December 31, 2003	$ 9,105

McGraw-Hill/Irwin   © 2004 The McGraw-Hill Companies

Slide 1-38

Relationship Among the Financial Statements

MAXIDRIVE CORP.
Balance Sheet
At December 31, 2003
(in thousands of dollars)

Assets	
Cash	$ 4,895
Accounts receivable	5,714
Inventories	8,517
Plant and equipment	7,154
Land	981
Total assets	$ 27,261
Liabilities and Stockholders' Equity	
Liabilities	
Accounts payable	$ 7,156
Notes payable	9,000
Total liabilities	$ 16,156
Stockholders' Equity	
Contributed capital	$ 2,000
Retained earnings	9,105
Total stockholders' equity	11,105
Total liabilities and stockholders' equity	$ 27,261

MAXIDRIVE CORP.
Statement of Cash Flows
For the Year Ended December 31, 2003
(in thousands of dollars)

Cash flows from operating activities:		
Cash collected from customers	$ 33,563	
Cash paid to suppliers and employees	(30,854)	
Cash paid for interest	(450)	
Cash paid for taxes	(1,190)	
Net cash flow from operating activities		$ 1,069
Cash flow from investing activities:		
Cash paid to purchase equipment	$ (1,625)	
Net cash flow from investing activities		(1,625)
Cash flow from financing activities:		
Cash received from bank loan	$ 1,400	
Cash paid for dividends	(1,000)	
Net cash flow from financing activities		400
Net decrease in cash during the year		$ (156)
Cash at beginning of the year		5,051
Cash at end of the year		$ 4,895

The change in cash on the statement of cash flows added to the beginning of the year balance in cash equals the ending balance in cash on the balance sheet.

McGraw-Hill/Irwin   © 2004 The McGraw-Hill Companies

Slide 1-39

Notes

❖ Notes provide supplemental information about the financial condition of a company.
❖ Three basic types of notes:
  ❖ Description of accounting rules applied.
  ❖ Presentation of additional detail about an item on the financial statements.
  ❖ Provides additional information about an item not on the financial statements.

McGraw-Hill/Irwin   © 2004 The McGraw-Hill Companies

1-40

Management Uses of Financial Statements

Marketing managers and credit managers use customers' financial statements to decide whether to extend credit.

Purchasing managers use suppliers' financial statements to decide whether suppliers have the resources to meet our demand for products.

Employees' union and human resource managers use the company's financial statements as a basis for contract negotiations over pay rates.

McGraw-Hill/Irwin © 2004 The McGraw-Hill Companies

1-41

Price/Earnings Ratio

$$\text{Price/Earnings Ratio} = \frac{\text{Market Price (of the Company)}}{\text{Net Income}}$$

This ratio is one method for estimating the value of a company.

McGraw-Hill/Irwin © 2004 The McGraw-Hill Companies

1-42

Responsibilities for the Accounting Communication Process

Effective communication means that the recipient understands what the sender intends to convey.

Decision makers need to understand accounting measurement rules.

McGraw-Hill/Irwin © 2004 The McGraw-Hill Companies

1-43

Generally Accepted Accounting Principles (GAAP)

Securities Act of 1933
Securities and Exchange Act of 1934

↓

The Securities and Exchange Commission (SEC) has been given broad powers to determine measurement rules for financial statements.

McGraw-Hill/Irwin   © 2004 The McGraw-Hill Companies

1-44

Generally Accepted Accounting Principles (GAAP)

The SEC has worked closely with the accounting profession to work out the detailed rules that have become known as GAAP.

↓

Currently, the Financial Accounting Standards Board (FASB) is recognized as the body to formulate GAAP.

McGraw-Hill/Irwin   © 2004 The McGraw-Hill Companies

1-45

Generally Accepted Accounting Principles (GAAP)

Companies incur the cost of preparing the financial statements and bear the following economic consequences . . .

❶ Effects on the selling price of stock.
❷ Effects on the amount of bonuses received by managers and other employees.
❸ Loss of competitive information to other companies.

McGraw-Hill/Irwin   © 2004 The McGraw-Hill Companies

1-46

Management Responsibility and the Demand for Auditing

To ensure the accuracy of the company's
financial information, management:

* Maintains a system of controls.
* Hires outside independent auditors.
* Forms a board of directors to review these two
  safeguards.

McGraw-Hill/Irwin   © 2004 The McGraw-Hill Companies

1-47

Independent Auditors

* Auditors express an
  opinion as to the
  fairness of the
  financial statement
  presentation.

Overall, I believe
these financial
statements are
fair.

* Independent auditors
  have responsibilities
  that extend to the
  general public.

McGraw-Hill/Irwin   © 2004 The McGraw-Hill Companies

1-48

Independent Auditors

An audit involves . . .

* Examining the financial reports to
  ensure compliance with GAAP.
* Examining the underlying
  transactions incorporated into
  the financial statements.
* Expressing an opinion as to the
  fairness of presentation of
  financial information.

McGraw-Hill/Irwin   © 2004 The McGraw-Hill Companies

1-49

Ethics, Reputation, and Legal Liability

The American Institute of Certified Public Accountants requires that all members adhere to a professional code of ethics.

McGraw-Hill/Irwin   © 2004 The McGraw-Hill Companies

1-50

Ethics, Reputation, and Legal Liability

A CPA's reputation for honesty and competence is his/her most important asset.

Like physicians, CPAs have liability for malpractice.

McGraw-Hill/Irwin   © 2004 The McGraw-Hill Companies

1-51

End of Chapter 1

McGraw-Hill/Irwin   © 2004 The McGraw-Hill Companies

Chapter 2

Investing and Financing Decisions
and the Balance Sheet

Business Background

To understand amounts appearing on a company's balance sheet we need to answer these questions:

(What business activities cause changes in the balance sheet?)
(How do specific activities affect each balance?)
(How do companies keep track of balance sheet amounts?)

McGraw-Hill/Irwin   © 2004 The McGraw-Hill Companies

The Conceptual Framework

Objective of External Financial Reporting
To provide useful economic information to external users for decision making and for assessing future cash flows.

Qualitative Characteristics	Elements of Statements
Relevancy	Asset
Reliability	Liability
Comparability	Stockholders' Equity
Consistency	Revenue
	Expense
	Gain
	Loss

McGraw-Hill/Irwin

2-4

The Conceptual Framework

Objective of External Financial Reporting
To provide useful economic information to external users for decision making and for assessing future cash flows.

Qualitative Characteristics	Primary Characteristics
Relevancy	•**Relevancy:** predictive value, feedback value, and timeliness.
Reliability	•**Reliability:** verifiability, representational faithfulness, and neutrality.
Comparability	
Consistency	**Secondary Characteristics**
	•**Comparability:** across companies.
	•**Consistency:** over time.

McGraw-Hill/Irwin

2-5

The Conceptual Framework

Asset: economic resource with probable future benefit.
Liability: probable future sacrifices of economic resources.
Stockholders' Equity: financing provided by owners and operations
Revenue: increase in assets or settlement of liabilities from ongoing operations.
Expense: decrease in assets or increase in liabilities from ongoing operations.
Gain: increase in assets or settlement of liabilities from peripheral activities.
Loss: decrease in assets or increase in liabilities from peripheral activities.

Financial Reporting
formation to external users
sessing future cash flows.

Elements of Statements

Asset

Liability

Stockholders' Equity

Revenue

Expense

Gain

Loss

2-6

The Conceptual Framework

Assumptions
Separate entity: Activities of the business are separate from activities of owners.
Continuity: The entity will not go out of business in the near future.
Unit-of-measure: Accounting measurements will be in the national monetary unit ($).
Time period: The long life of a company can be reported over a series of shorter time periods.

McGraw-Hill/Irwin   © 2004 The McGraw-Hill Companies

The Conceptual Framework

Principles

Historical cost: Cash equivalent cost given up is the basis for initial recording of elements.

Revenue recognition: Record when measurable, realizable (transaction takes place and collection probable), and earned (substantially accomplished what is necessary to be entitled to benefits).

Matching: Record expenses when incurred in earning revenue.

Full disclosure: Provide information sufficiently important to influence a decision.

McGraw-Hill/Irwin   © 2004 The McGraw-Hill Companies

The Conceptual Framework

Constraints

Cost-benefit: Benefits to users should outweigh costs of providing information.

Materiality: Relatively small amounts not likely to influence decisions are to be recorded in most cost beneficial way.

Industry peculiarities: Industry specific measurements and reporting deviations may be acceptable.

Conservatism: Exercise care not to overstate assets and revenues or understate liabilities and expenses.

McGraw-Hill/Irwin   © 2004 The McGraw-Hill Companies

Nature of Business Transactions

External events: exchanges of assets and liabilities between the business and one or more other parties.

Borrow cash
from the bank

McGraw-Hill/Irwin   © 2004 The McGraw-Hill Companies

2-10

Nature of Business Transactions

Internal events: not an exchange between the business and other parties, but have a direct effect on the accounting entity.

Loss due to fire damage.

McGraw-Hill/Irwin — © 2004 The McGraw-Hill Companies

2-11

Accounts

An organized format used by companies to accumulate the dollar effects of transactions.

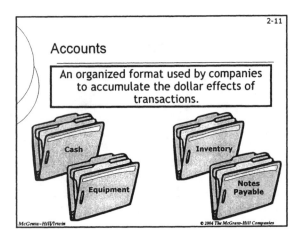

Cash Inventory Equipment Notes Payable

McGraw-Hill/Irwin — © 2004 The McGraw-Hill Companies

2-12

Accounts

An organized format used by companies to accumulate the dollar effects of transactions.

While U.S. companies follow GAAP to prepare their financial statements, other countries have significant variations from the accounting and reporting rules of GAAP.

Some countries use different account titles from U.S. companies.

Principles of Transaction Analysis

♦ Every transaction affects at least two accounts (duality of effects).
♦ The accounting equation must remain in balance after each transaction.

A = L + SE

Duality of Effects

Most transactions with external parties involve an exchange where the business entity both gives up something and receives something in return.

Balancing the Accounting Equation

• Accounts and effects
  ▪ Identify the accounts affected and classify them by type of account (A, L, SE).
  ▪ Determine the direction of the efect (increase or decrease) on each account.
• Balancing
  ▪ Verify that the accounting equation (A = L + SE) remains in balance.

Balancing the Accounting Equation

Let's see how we keep the accounting equation in balance for Papa John's.

All amounts are in thousands of dollars.

McGraw-Hill/Irwin   © 2004 The McGraw-Hill Companies

Papa John's issues $2,000 of additional common stock to new investors for cash.

Identify & Classify the Accounts
1. Cash (asset)
2. Contributed Capital (equity)

Determine the Direction of the Effect
1. Cash increases.
2. Contributed Capital increases.

McGraw-Hill/Irwin   © 2004 The McGraw-Hill Companies

Papa John's issues $2,000 of additional common stock to new investors for cash.

	Cash	Investments	Equip.	Notes Receivable		Notes Payable	Contributed Capital	Retained Earnings
(a)	2,000						2,000	
Effect		2,000			=		2,000	

A = L + SE

McGraw-Hill/Irwin   © 2004 The McGraw-Hill Companies

The company borrows $6,000 from the local bank, signing a three-year note.

Identify & Classify the Accounts
1. Cash (asset)
2. Notes Payable (liability)

Determine the Direction of the Effect
1. Cash increases.
2. Notes Payable increases.

McGraw-Hill/Irwin   © 2004 The McGraw-Hill Companies

The company borrows $6,000 from the local bank, signing a three-year note.

	Cash	Investments	Equip.	Notes Receivable	Notes Payable	Contributed Capital	Retained Earnings
(a)	2,000					2,000	
(b)	6,000				6,000		
Effect	8,000			=	8,000		

A = L + SE

McGraw-Hill/Irwin   © 2004 The McGraw-Hill Companies

Papa John's purchases $10,000 of new equipment, paying $2,000 in cash and signing a two-year note payable for the rest.

Identify & Classify the Accounts
1. Equipment (asset)
2. Cash (asset)
3. Notes Payable (liability)

Determine the Direction of the Effect
1. Equipment increases.
2. Cash decreases.
3. Notes Payable increases.

McGraw-Hill/Irwin   © 2004 The McGraw-Hill Companies

Slide 2-22

Papa John's purchases $10,000 of new equipment, paying $2,000 in cash and signing a two-year note payable for the rest.

	Cash	Investments	Equip.	Notes Receivable		Notes Payable	Contributed Capital	Retained Earnings
(a)	2,000						2,000	
(b)	6,000					6,000		
(c)	(2,000)		10,000			8,000		
Effect		16,000			=	16,000		

A = L + SE

Slide 2-23

Papa John's lends $3,000 to new franchisees who sign five-year notes agreeing to repay the loan.

Identify & Classify the Accounts
1. Cash (asset)
2. Notes Receivable (asset)

Determine the Direction of the Effect
1. Cash decreases.
2. Notes Receivable increases.

Slide 2-24

Papa John's lends $3,000 to new franchisees who sign five-year notes agreeing to repay the loan.

	Cash	Investments	Equip.	Notes Receivable		Notes Payable	Contributed Capital	Retained Earnings
(a)	2,000						2,000	
(b)	6,000					6,000		
(c)	(2,000)		10,000			8,000		
(d)	(3,000)			3,000				
Effect		16,000			=	16,000		

A = L + SE

Papa John's purchases $1,000 of stock in other companies as an investment.

Identify & Classify the Accounts
1. Cash (asset)
2. Investments (asset)

Determine the Direction of the Effect
1. Cash decreases.
2. Investments increase.

Papa John's purchases $1,000 of stock in other companies as an investment.

	Cash	Investments	Equip.	Notes Receivable	Notes Payable	Contributed Capital	Retained Earnings
(a)	2,000					2,000	
(b)	6,000				6,000		
(c)	(2,000)		10,000		8,000		
(d)	(3,000)			3,000			
(e)	(1,000)	1,000					
Effect		16,000			=	16,000	

A = L + SE

Papa John's board of directors declares and pays $3,000 in dividends to shareholders.

Identify & Classify the Accounts
1. Cash (asset)
2. Retained Earnings (equity)

Determine the Direction of the Effect
1. Cash decreases.
2. Retained Earnings decreases.

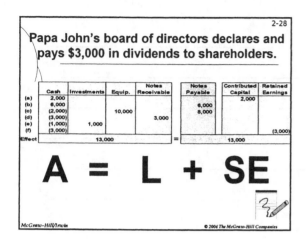

Slide 2-28:

Papa John's board of directors declares and pays $3,000 in dividends to shareholders.

	Cash	Investments	Equip.	Notes Receivable		Notes Payable	Contributed Capital	Retained Earnings
(a)	2,000						2,000	
(b)	6,000					6,000		
(c)	(2,000)		10,000			8,000		
(d)	(3,000)			3,000				
(e)	(1,000)	1,000						
(f)	(3,000)							(3,000)
Effect		13,000			=		13,000	

A = L + SE

McGraw-Hill/Irwin © 2004 The McGraw-Hill Companies

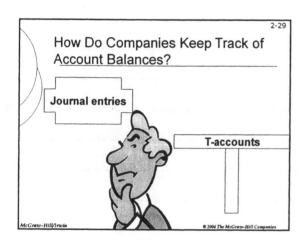

Slide 2-29:

How Do Companies Keep Track of Account Balances?

Journal entries

T-accounts

McGraw-Hill/Irwin © 2004 The McGraw-Hill Companies

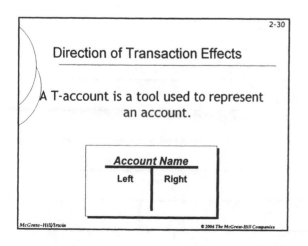

Slide 2-30:

Direction of Transaction Effects

A T-account is a tool used to represent an account.

Account Name	
Left	Right

McGraw-Hill/Irwin © 2004 The McGraw-Hill Companies

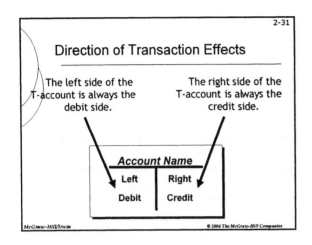

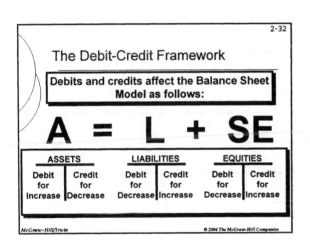

The Debit-Credit Framework

A = L + SE

ASSETS		LIABILITIES		EQUITIES	
Debit for Increase	Credit for Decrease	Debit for Decrease	Credit for Increase	Debit for Decrease	Credit for Increase

Remember that Stockholders' Equity includes Contributed Capital and Retained Earnings.

Analytical Tool: The Journal Entry

A typical journal looks like this:

GENERAL JOURNAL				Page 1
Date	Account Titles and Explanation	Posted Ref.	Debit	Credit

McGraw-Hill/Irwin © 2004 The McGraw-Hill Companies

Analytical Tool: The Journal Entry

A journal entry might look like this:

GENERAL JOURNAL				Page 1
Date	Account Titles and Explanation	Posted Ref.	Debit	Credit
Jan. 1	Cash		20,000	
	Contributed Capital			20,000

McGraw-Hill/Irwin © 2004 The McGraw-Hill Companies

Analytical Tool: The Journal Entry

Provide a reference date for each transaction.

Debits are written first.

GENERAL JOURNAL				Page 1
Date	Account Titles and Explanation	Posted Ref.	Debit	Credit
Jan. 1	Cash		20,000	
	Contributed Capital			20,000

Credits are indented and written after debits.

Total debits must equal total credits.

McGraw-Hill/Irwin © 2004 The McGraw-Hill Companies

Analytical Tool: The T-Account

After journal entries are prepared, the accountant posts (transfers) the dollar amounts to each account that was affected by the transaction.

GENERAL JOURNAL				Page 1
Date	Account Titles and Explanation	Posted Ref.	Debit	Credit
Jan. 1	Cash		20,000	
	Contributed Capital			20,000

Post → Ledger

McGraw-Hill/Irwin   © 2004 The McGraw-Hill Companies

Transaction Analysis Illustrated

Let's prepare some journal entries for Papa John's and post them to the ledger.

McGraw-Hill/Irwin   © 2004 The McGraw-Hill Companies

Papa John's issues $2,000 of additional common stock to new investors for cash.

GENERAL JOURNAL				Page 1
Date	Account Titles and Explanation	Posted Ref.	Debit	Credit
	Cash		2,000	
	Contributed Capital			2,000

Cash			
Beg. Bal.	6,000		
(a)	2,000		
	8,000		

Contributed Capital			
		1,000	Beg. Bal.
		2,000	(a)
		3,000	

McGraw-Hill/Irwin   © 2004 The McGraw-Hill Companies

The company borrows $6,000 from the local bank, signing a one-year note.

GENERAL JOURNAL				Page 1
Date	Account Titles and Explanation	Posted Ref.	Debit	Credit
	Cash		6,000	
	Notes Payable			6,000

Cash

Beg. Bal.	6,000		
(a)	2,000		
(b)	6,000		
	14,000		

Notes Payable

		146,000	Beg. Bal.
		6,000	(b)
		152,000	

McGraw-Hill/Irwin © 2004 The McGraw-Hill Companies

Papa John's purchases $10,000 of new equipment, paying $2,000 in cash and signing a two-year note payable for the rest.

GENERAL JOURNAL				Page 1
Date	Account Titles and Explanation	Posted Ref.	Debit	Credit
	Equipment		10,000	
	Cash			2,000
	Notes Payable			8,000

Let's see how to post this entry . . .

McGraw-Hill/Irwin © 2004 The McGraw-Hill Companies

Papa John's purchases $10,000 of new equipment, paying $2,000 in cash and signing a two-year note payable for the rest.

Equipment

Beg. Bal.	246,000		
(c)	10,000		
	256,000		

Cash

Beg. Bal.	6,000		
(a)	2,000	2,000	(c)
(b)	6,000		
	12,000		

Notes Payable

		146,000	Beg. Bal.
		6,000	(b)
		8,000	(c)
		160,000	

McGraw-Hill/Irwin © 2004 The McGraw-Hill Companies

Balance Sheet Preparation

It is possible to prepare a balance sheet at any point in time from the balances in the accounts.

McGraw-Hill/Irwin © 2004 The McGraw-Hill Companies

PAPA JOHN'S INTERNATIONAL, INC. AND SUBSIDIARIES
Consolidated Balance Sheets
January 31, 2001
(dollars in thousands)

These balances come from Papa John's ledger accounts on January 31, 2001.

Assets		
Current assets		
Cash and cash equivalents	$	5,000
Short-term investments		7,000
Accounts receivable		23,000
Inventories		18,000
Prepaid expenses		7,000
Other current assets		6,000
Total current assets		66,000
Net property and equipment		256,000
Notes receivable		20,000
Intangibles		48,000
Other assets		18,000
Total assets	$	409,000
Liabilities and Stockholders' Equity		
Current liabilities		
Accounts payable	$	24,000
Accrued expenses payable		45,000
Other current liabilities		1,000
Total current liabilities		70,000
Unearned franchise fees		6,000
Long-term notes payable		160,000
Other long-term liabilities		8,000
Stockholders' equity		
Contributed capital		3,000
Retained earnings		162,000
Total stockholders' equity		165,000
Total liabilities and stockholders' equity	$	409,000

McGraw-Hill/Irwin

Focus on Cash Flows

Investing Activities	Effect on Cash Flows
Purchasing long-term assets for cash	-
Selling long-term assets for cash	+
Lending cash to others	-
Receiving principal payments in cash on loans to others	+

Financing Activities	Effect on Cash Flows
Borrowing cash from banks	+
Repaying the principal on loans to banks	-
Issuing stock for cash	+
Repurchasing stock with cash	-
Paying cash dividends	-

McGraw-Hill/Irwin

Chapter 3

Operating Decisions and the Income Statement

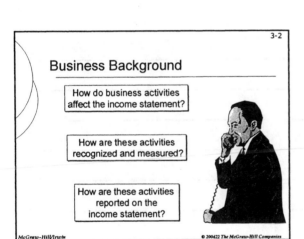

Business Background

How do business activities affect the income statement?

How are these activities recognized and measured?

How are these activities reported on the income statement?

McGraw-Hill/Irwin © 200422 The McGraw-Hill Companies

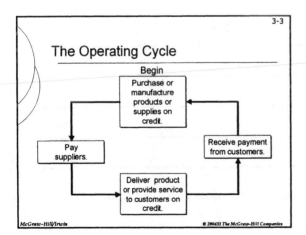

The Operating Cycle

Begin

Purchase or manufacture products or supplies on credit.

Pay suppliers.

Receive payment from customers.

Deliver product or provide service to customers on credit.

McGraw-Hill/Irwin © 200433 The McGraw-Hill Companies

3-4

Underlying Accounting Assumptions

Time Period: The long life of a company can be reported over a series of shorter time periods.

Recognition Issues : When should the effects of operating activities be recognized (recorded)?

Measurement Issues: What amounts should be recognized?

McGraw-Hill/Irwin
© 2004 The McGraw-Hill Companies

3-5

The Time Period Assumption

To meet the needs of decision makers, we report financial information for relatively short time periods (monthly, quarterly, annually).

Life of the Business

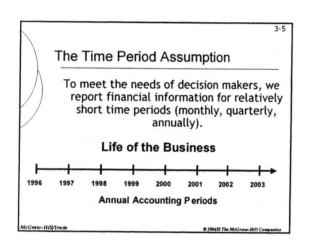

1996   1997   1998   1999   2000   2001   2002   2003

Annual Accounting Periods

McGraw-Hill/Irwin
© 2004 The McGraw-Hill Companies

3-6

Elements on the Income Statement

Revenue
Increases in assets or settlement of liabilities from ongoing operations.

Expense
Decreases in assets or increases in liabilities from ongoing operations.

Gains
Increase in assets or settlement of liabilities from peripheral transactions.

Losses
Decreases in assets or increases in liabilities from peripheral transactions.

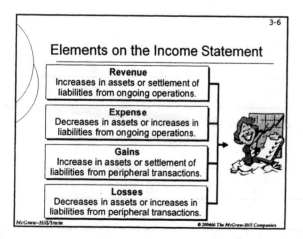

McGraw-Hill/Irwin
© 2004 The McGraw-Hill Companies

Slide 1

Papa John's Primary Operating Activities

- Sell pizza
- Sell franchises

PAPA JOHN'S INTERNATIONAL, INC. AND SUBSIDIARIES	
Consolidated Statement of Income	
For the Year Ended December 31, 2000	
(In thousands)	
Revenues	
Restaurant sales	$ 886,000
Franchise royalties and development fees	59,000
Total revenues	945,000
Costs and expenses	
Cost of sales	416,000
Salaries and benefits	155,000
Rent expense	23,000
Advertising expense	42,000
General and administrative expenses	72,000
Depreciation expense	34,000
Other operating costs	118,000
Total costs and expenses	860,000
Operating income	85,000
Other revenues and gains (expense and losses)	
Investment income	2,000
Interest expense	(8,000)
Losses due to asset impairment and litigation	(27,000)
Income before income taxes	52,000
Income tax expense	20,000
Net income	$ 32,000
Earnings per share	$ 1.29

McGraw-Hill/Irwin

Slide 2

Papa John's Primary Operating Expenses

- Cost of sales (used inventory)
- Salaries and benefits to employees
- Other costs (like advertising, insurance, and depreciation)

PAPA JOHN'S INTERNATIONAL, INC. AND SUBSIDIARIES	
Consolidated Statement of Income	
For the Year Ended December 31, 2000	
(In thousands)	
Revenues	
Restaurant sales	$ 886,000
Franchise royalties and development fees	59,000
Total revenues	945,000
Costs and expenses	
Cost of sales	416,000
Salaries and benefits	155,000
Rent expense	23,000
Advertising expense	42,000
General and administrative expenses	72,000
Depreciation expense	34,000
Other operating costs	118,000
Total costs and expenses	860,000
Operating income	85,000
Other revenues and gains (expense and losses)	
Investment income	2,000
Interest expense	(8,000)
Losses due to asset impairment and litigation	(27,000)
Income before income taxes	52,000
Income tax expense	20,000
Net income	$ 32,000
Earnings per share	$ 1.29

McGraw-Hill/Irwin

Slide 3

Corporations are taxable entities. Income tax expense is *Income Before Income Taxes × Tax Rate* (Federal, State, Local and Foreign).

PAPA JOHN'S INTERNATIONAL, INC. AND SUBSIDIARIES	
Consolidated Statement of Income	
For the Year Ended December 31, 2000	
(In thousands)	
Revenues	
Restaurant sales	$ 886,000
Franchise royalties and development fees	59,000
Total revenues	945,000
Costs and expenses	
Cost of sales	416,000
Salaries and benefits	155,000
Rent expense	23,000
Advertising expense	42,000
General and administrative expenses	72,000
Depreciation expense	34,000
Other operating costs	118,000
Total costs and expenses	860,000
Operating income	85,000
Other revenues and gains (expense and losses)	
Investment income	2,000
Interest expense	(8,000)
Losses due to asset impairment and litigation	(27,000)
Income before income taxes	52,000
Income tax expense	20,000
Net income	$ 32,000
Earnings per share	$ 1.29

McGraw-Hill/Irwin

PAPA JOHN'S INTERNATIONAL, INC. AND SUBSIDIARIES	
Consolidated Statement of Income	
For the Year Ended December 31, 2000	
(In thousands)	
Revenues	
Restaurant sales	$ 886,000
Franchise royalties and development fees	59,000
Total revenues	945,000
Costs and expenses	
Cost of sales	416,000
Salaries and benefits	155,000
Rent expense	23,000
Advertising expense	42,000
General and administrative expenses	72,000
Depreciation expense	34,000
Other operating costs	118,000
Total costs and expenses	860,000
Operating income	85,000
Other revenues and gains (expense and losses)	
Investment income	2,000
Interest expense	(8,000)
Losses due to asset impairment and litigation	(27,000)
Income before income taxes	52,000
Income tax expense	20,000
Net income	$ 32,000
Earnings per share	$ 1.29

Earnings Per Share

$$\frac{\text{Net Income}}{\text{Weighted Average Number of Common Shares Outstanding}}$$

McGraw-Hill/Irwin

Cash Basis Accounting

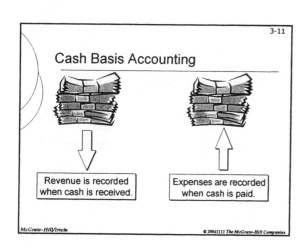

Revenue is recorded when cash is received.	Expenses are recorded when cash is paid.

McGraw-Hill/Irwin   © 20041111 The McGraw-Hill Companies

Accrual Accounting

Assets, liabilities, revenues, and expenses should be recognized when the transaction that causes them occurs, *not necessarily when cash is paid or received.*

Required by -

Generally
Acceptable
Accounting
Principles

GAAP

McGraw-   © 20041212 The McGraw-Hill Companies

Revenue Principle

Recognize revenues when . . .

- Delivery has occurred or services have been rendered.
- There is persuasive evidence of an arrangement for customer payment.
- The price is fixed or determinable.
- Collection is reasonably assured.

Revenue Principle

If cash is received before the company delivers goods or services, the liability account *UNEARNED REVENUE* is recorded.

Cash received before revenue is earned -

$ Received →

| Cash (+A) | x,xxx | |
| Unearned revenue (+L) | | x,xxx |

Revenue Principle

If cash is received before the company delivers goods or services, the liability account *UNEARNED REVENUE* is recorded.

Cash received before revenue is earned -

$ Received   Company Delivers →

| Cash (+A) | x,xxx | |
| Unearned revenue (+L) | | x,xxx |

| Unearned Revenue (-L) | x,xxx | |
| Fee Revenue (+R) | | x,xxx |

Revenue Principle

Typical liabilities that become
revenue when earned include . . .

CASH COLLECTED (Goods or services due to customers)	over time will become	REVENUE (Earned when goods or services provided)
Rent collected in advance	→	Rent revenue
Unearned air traffic revenue	→	Air traffic revenue
Deferred subscription revenue	→	Subscription revenue

McGraw-Hill/Irwin   © 20041616 The McGraw-Hill Companies

Revenue Principle

When cash is received on the date
the revenue is earned, the
following entry is made:

Company
Delivers
AND
$
Received

| Cash (+A) | x,xxx | |
| Fee revenue (+R) | | x,xxx |

McGraw-Hill/Irwin   © 20041717 The McGraw-Hill Companies

Revenue Principle

If cash is received after the company
delivers goods or services, an as set
ACCOUNTS RECEIVABLE is recorded.

Cash received after revenue is earned -

Company
Delivers

| Accounts receivable (+A) | x,xxx | |
| Fee revenue (+R) | | x,xxx |

McGraw-Hill/Irwin   © 20041818 The McGraw-Hill Companies

Revenue Principle

> If cash is received after the company delivers goods or services, an as set *ACCOUNTS RECEIVABLE* is recorded.

Cash received after revenue is earned -

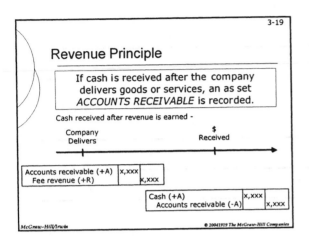

| Accounts receivable (+A) | x,xxx | |
| Fee revenue (+R) | | x,xxx |

| | Cash (+A) | x,xxx | |
| | Accounts receivable (-A) | | x,xxx |

McGraw-Hill/Irwin © 20041919 The McGraw-Hill Companies

The Revenue Principle

Assets reflecting revenues earned but not yet received in cash include . . .

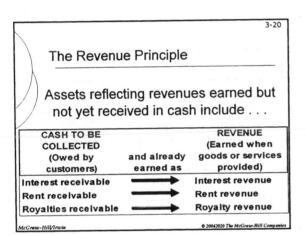

CASH TO BE COLLECTED (Owed by customers)	and already earned as	REVENUE (Earned when goods or services provided)
Interest receivable	➔	Interest revenue
Rent receivable	➔	Rent revenue
Royalties receivable	➔	Royalty revenue

McGraw-Hill/Irwin © 20042020 The McGraw-Hill Companies

The Matching Principle

> Resources consumed to earn revenues in an accounting period should be recorded in that period, *regardless of when cash is paid*.

McGraw-Hill/Irwin © 20042121 The McGraw-Hill Companies

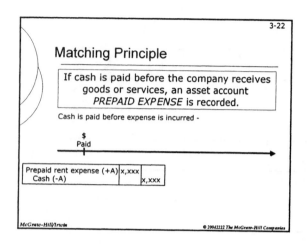

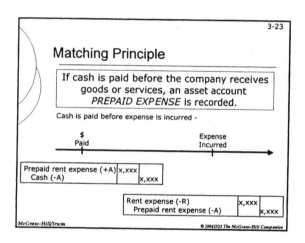

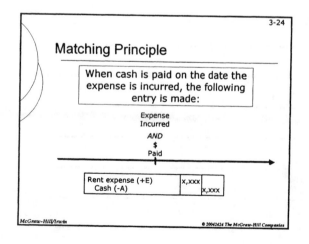

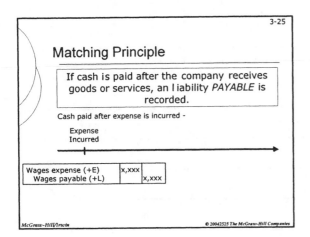

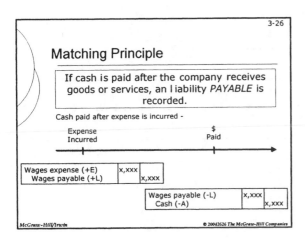

Matching Principle

Typical assets and their related expense accounts include. . .

CASH PAID FOR	as used over time becomes	EXPENSE
Supplies Inventory	➡	Supplies expense
Prepaid Insurance	➡	Insurance expense
Buildings and equipment	➡	Depreciation expense

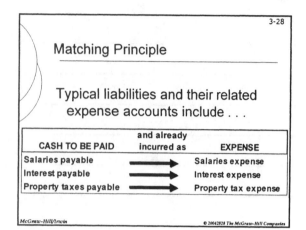

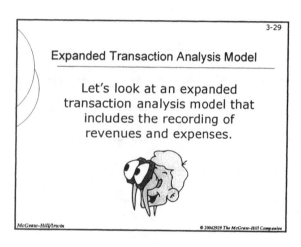

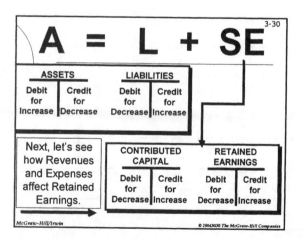

3-11

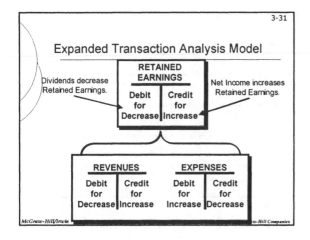

Expanded Transaction Analysis Model

3-31

RETAINED EARNINGS

Dividends decrease Retained Earnings.

Net Income increases Retained Earnings.

Debit for Decrease	Credit for Increase

REVENUES		EXPENSES	
Debit for Decrease	Credit for Increase	Debit for Increase	Credit for Decrease

McGraw-Hill/Irwin   w-Hill Companies

3-32

Analyzing Papa John's Transaction

Let's apply the complete transaction analysis model to some of Papa John's transactions.

All amounts are in thousands of dollars.

McGraw-Hill/Irwin   © 20043232 The McGraw-Hill Companies

3-33

Papa John's sold franchises for $400 cash. The company earned $100 immediately. The rest will be earned over several months.

Identify & Classify the Accounts
1. **Cash (asset)**
2. **Franchise fee revenue (revenue)**
3. **Unearned franchise fees (liability)**

Determine the Direction of the Effect
1. **Cash increases.**
2. **Franchise fee revenue increases.**
3. **Unearned franchise fees increases.**

McGraw-Hill/Irwin   © 20043333 The McGraw-Hill Companies

Papa John's sold franchises for $400 cash. The [3-34]
company earned $100 immediately. The rest will
be earned over several months.

Assets	=	Liabilities	+	Stockholders' Equity	
Cash	400	Unearned franchise revenue	300	Franchise fees revenue	100

GENERAL JOURNAL			Page 1	
Date	Description	Debit	Credit
	Cash	400	
	Unearned franchise revenue		300
	Franchise fees revenue		100

© 20043434 The McGraw-Hill Companies

The company sold $36,000 of pizzas for cash. [3-35]
The costs of the pizza ingredients for those
sales were $9,600.

Identify & Classify the Accounts
1. Cash (asset)
2. Restaurant sales revenue (revenue)
3. Cost of sales- restaurant (expense)
4. Inventories (asset)

Determine the Direction of the Effect
1. Cash increases.
2. Restaurant sales revenue increases.
3. Cost of sales- restaurant increases.
4. Inventories decrease.

The company received $35,200 for pizza sales. [3-36]
The cost of the pizza ingredients for those sales
was $9,600.

Assets	=	Liabilities	+	Stockholders' Equity	
Cash	36,000			Restaurant sales revenue	36,000
Inventory	(9,600)			Cost of sales	(9,600)

GENERAL JOURNAL			Page 1	
Date	Description	Debit	Credit
	Cash	36,000	
	Restaurant sales revenue		36,000
	Cost of sales - restaurant	9,600	
	Inventories		9,600

© 20043636 The McGraw-Hill Companies

How are Unadjusted Financial Statements Prepared?

After posting all of the January transactions to T-accounts, we can prepare Papa John's unadjusted financial statements.

Several expenses, including income tax expense, have not determined at this point in the accounting process.

PAPA JOHN'S INTERNATIONAL, INC. AND SUBSIDIARIES
Unadjusted Consolidated Statement of Income
For the Month Ended Janaury 31, 2001
(Dollars in thousands)

Revenues	
Restaurant and commissary sales	$ 66,000
Franchise fees	2,800
Total revenues	68,800
Costs and expenses	
Cost of sales	30,000
Salaries and benefits expense	14,000
Rent expense	-
Advertising expense	-
General and administrative expenses	7,000
Depreciation and amortizaation expense	-
Other operating costs	-
Total costs and expenses	51,000
Operating income	17,800
Other revneues and gains (expenses and losses)	
Investment income	1,000
Interest expense	-
Gain on sale of land	3,000
Income before income taxes	21,800
Income tax expense	-
Net income	$ 21,800
Earnings per share (for the month)	$ 0.88

Unadjusted Statement of Retained Earnings

PAPA JOHN'S INTERNATIONAL, INC. AND SUBSIDIARIES
Unadjusted Consolidated Statement of Retained Earnings
For the Month Ended Janaury 31, 2001
(Dollars in thousands)

Beginning balance, December 30, 2000	$ 165,000
Unadjusted net income	21,800
Dividends	(3,000)
Ending balance, January 31, 2001	$ 183,800

The unadjusted net income comes from the Income Statement just prepared.

Slide 1

Unadjusted Balance Sheet

The ending balance from the Statement of Retained Earnings flows into the equity section of the Balance Sheet.

PAPA JOHN'S INTERNATIONAL, INC. AND SUBSIDIARIES
Unadjusted Consolidated Balance Sheets
(Dollars in thousands)

Assets	1/31/01
Current assets:	
Cash	$ 33,900
Short-term investments	7,000
Accounts receivable	19,200
Inventories	17,000
Prepaid expenses	16,000
Other current assets	6,000
Total current assets	99,100
Property and equipment, net of depreciation	255,000
Notes receivable	20,000
Intangibles	49,000
Other assets	18,000
Total assets	$ 441,100
Liabilities and Stockholders' Equity	
Current liabilities:	
Accounts payable	$ 34,000
Accrued expenses payable	45,000
Other current liabilities	1,000
Total current liabilities	80,000
Unearned franchise fees	6,300
Long-term notes payable	160,000
Other long-term liabilities	8,000
Total liabilities	254,300
Stockholders' equity:	
Contributed capital	3,000
Retained earnings	183,800
Total stockholders' equity	186,800
Total liabilities and stockholders' equity	$ 441,100

McGraw-Hill/Irwin

Slide 2

Focus on Cash Flows

Nature of Operating Activity		Effect on Cash Flows
Cash received from:	Customers	+
	Investments	+
Cash paid to:	Suppliers	-
	Employees	-
	Interest paid	-
	Income taxes paid	-

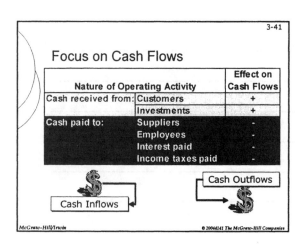

Cash Inflows

Cash Outflows

McGraw-Hill/Irwin © 20044141 The McGraw-Hill Companies

Slide 3

PAPA JOHN'S INTERNATIONAL, INC. AND SUBSIDIARIES
Unadjusted Consolidated Statement of Cash Flows
For the Month Ended January 31, 2001
(Dollars in thousands)

Operating Activities		
Cash from: Customers	$	69,000
Franchises		3,900
Interest on investments		1,000
Cash to: Suppliers		(35,000)
Employees		(14,000)
Net cash provided by operating activities		24,900
Investing Activities		
Sold land		4,000
Purchased property and equipment		(2,000)
Purchased investments		(1,000)
Lent funds to franchisees		(3,000)
Net cash used in investing activities		(2,000)
Financing Activities		
Issued common stock		2,000
Borrowed from banks		6,000
Paid dividends		(3,000)
Net cash provided by financing activities		5,000
Net increase in cash		27,900
Cash at beginning of month		6,000
Cash at end of month	$	33,900

The ending cash balance agrees with the amount on the Balance Sheet.

McGraw-Hill/Irwin

Financial Analysis

Asset Turnover Ratio	=	Sales (or Operating) Revenues
		Average Total Assets

Measures the sales generated per dollar of assets.

Creditors and analysts used this ratio to assess a company's effectiveness at controlling current and noncurrent assets.

McGraw-Hill/Irwin
© 20044343 The McGraw-Hill Companies

Financial Analysis

Reporting financial information by geographic and operating segments.

Papa John's Notes to Consolidated Financial Statements

Note 19 Segment Information (in thousands)	2000	1999	1998
Revenue from external customers:			
Domestic restaurants	$ 456,637	$ 394,636	$ 344,089
Domestic commissaries	351,255	306,909	255,083
Domestic franchising	52,704	47,078	37,445
International	30,848	3,624	131
All others	53,233	53,078	45,404
Total revenues from external customers	$ 944,677	$ 805,325	$ 682,152

McGraw-Hill/Irwin
© 20044444 The McGraw-Hill Companies

End of Chapter 3

McGraw-Hill/Irwin
© 20044545 The McGraw-Hill Companies

Chapter 4

Adjustments, Financial Statements, and the Quality of Earnings

---

Business Background

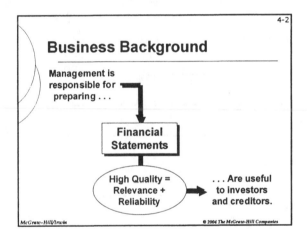

Management is responsible for preparing . . .

Financial Statements

High Quality = Relevance + Reliability

. . . Are useful to investors and creditors.

McGraw-Hill/Irwin © 2004 The McGraw-Hill Companies

Business Background

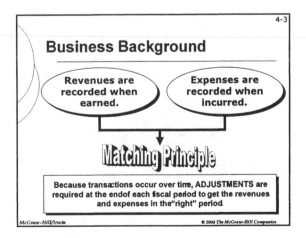

Revenues are recorded when earned.

Expenses are recorded when incurred.

Matching Principle

Because transactions occur over time, ADJUSTMENTS are required at the end of each fiscal period to get the revenues and expenses in the "right" period.

McGraw-Hill/Irwin © 2004 The McGraw-Hill Companies

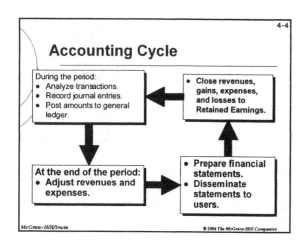

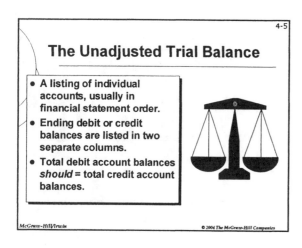

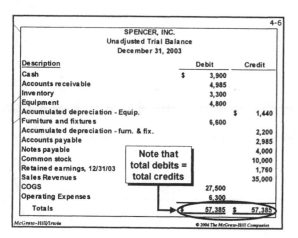

SPENCER, INC.
Unadjusted Trial Balance
December 31, 2003

Description	Debit	Credit
Cash	$ 3,900	
Accounts receivable	4,985	
Inventory	3,300	
Equipment	4,800	
Accumulated depreciation - equip.		$ 1,440
Furniture and fixtures	6,600	
Accumulated depreciation - furn. & fix.		2,200
Accounts payable		2,985
Notes payable		|000
Common stock		|000
Retained earnings, 12/31/03		760
Sales Revenues		|000
COGS		
Operating Expenses		
Totals	$ 57,385	$ 57,385

Accumulated depreciation is a contra-asset account. It is directly related to an asset account but has the opposite balance.

McGraw-Hill/Irwin © 2004 The McGraw-Hill Companies

SPENCER, INC.
Unadjusted Trial Balance
December 31, 2003

Description	Debit	Credit
Cash	$ 3,900	
Accounts receivable	4,985	
Inventory	3,300	
Equipment	4,800	
Accumulated depreciation - Equip.		$ 1,440
Furniture and fixtures	6,600	
A		2,200
A		2,985
N		4,000
Common stock		10,000
Retained earnings, 12/31/03		1,760
Sales Revenues		35,000
COGS	27,500	
Operating Expenses	6,300	
Totals	$ 57,385	$ 57,385

Cost - Accumulated depreciation = BOOK VALUE.

McGraw-Hill/Irwin © 2004 The McGraw-Hill Companies

The Unadjusted Trial Balance

If total debits do not equal total credits on the trial balance, errors have occurred . . .

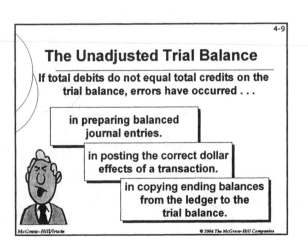

in preparing balanced journal entries.

in posting the correct dollar effects of a transaction.

in copying ending balances from the ledger to the trial balance.

McGraw-Hill/Irwin © 2004 The McGraw-Hill Companies

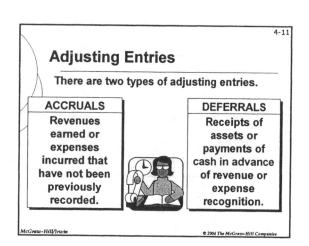

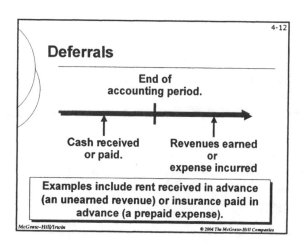

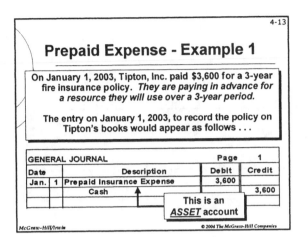

Prepaid Expense - Example 1

On January 1, 2003, Tipton, Inc. paid $3,600 for a 3-year fire insurance policy. *They are paying in advance for a resource they will use over a 3-year period.*

The entry on January 1, 2003, to record the policy on Tipton's books would appear as follows . . .

GENERAL JOURNAL			Page	1
Date		Description	Debit	Credit
Jan.	1	Prepaid Insurance Expense	3,600	
		Cash		3,600

This is an *ASSET* account

McGraw-Hill/Irwin   © 2004 The McGraw-Hill Companies

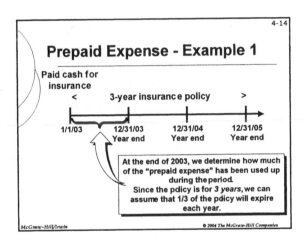

Prepaid Expense - Example 1

Paid cash for insurance

< 3-year insurance policy >

1/1/03   12/31/03   12/31/04   12/31/05
          Year end   Year end   Year end

At the end of 2003, we determine how much of the "prepaid expense" has been used up during the period.
Since the policy is for *3 years*, we can assume that 1/3 of the policy will expire each year.

McGraw-Hill/Irwin   © 2004 The McGraw-Hill Companies

Prepaid Expense - Example 1

On *December 31, 2003*, Tipton must adjust the Prepaid Insurance Expense account to reflect that 1 year of the policy has expired.

$3,600 × 1/3 = $1,200 per year.

GENERAL JOURNAL			Page	365
Date		Description	Debit	Credit
Dec	31	Insurance Expense	1,200	
		Prepaid Insurance Exp.		1,200

In effect, the prepaid asset goes down, while the expense goes up.

McGraw-Hill/Irwin   © 2004 The McGraw-Hill Companies

Prepaid Expense - Example 1

After we post the entry to the T-accounts, the account balances look like this:

Prepaid Insurance Expense		Insurance Expense	
1/1 3,600	12/31 1,200	12/31 1,200	
Bal. 2,400		Bal. 1,200	

McGraw-Hill/Irwin   © 2004 The McGraw-Hill Companies

Deferrals

Now, let's look at an example of cash received in advance.

McGraw-Hill/Irwin   © 2004 The McGraw-Hill Companies

Unearned Revenue - Example 2

On December 1, 2003, Tom's Rentals received a check for $3,000, for the first four months' rent of a new tenant.

The entry on December 1, 2003, to record the receipt of the prepaid rent payment would be . . .

GENERAL JOURNAL			Page	1
Date	Description		Debit	Credit
Dec 1	Cash		3,000	
	Unearned Rent Revenue			3,000

This is a *LIABILITY* account

McGraw-Hill/Irwin   © 2004 The McGraw-Hill Companies

Unearned Revenue - Example 2

Received
cash for rent

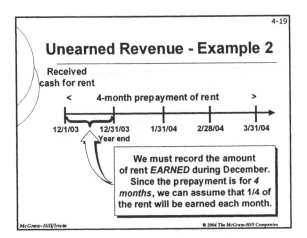

< 4-month prepayment of rent >

12/1/03   12/31/03   1/31/04   2/28/04   3/31/04
          Year end

We must record the amount
of rent *EARNED* during December.
Since the prepayment is for *4
months*, we can assume that 1/4 of
the rent will be earned each month.

McGraw-Hill/Irwin   © 2004 The McGraw-Hill Companies

Unearned Revenue - Example 2

On *December 31, 2003*, Tom's Rentals must adjust the
Unearned Rent Revenue account to reflect that 1
month of rent revenue has been earned.

$3,000 × 1/4 = $750 per month.

GENERAL JOURNAL		Page	365
Date	Description	Debit	Credit
Dec 31	Unearned Rent Revenue	750	
	Rent Revenue		750

In effect, our obligation to let them occupy the space for a
period of has decreased, because they used the space for 1
month.

McGraw-Hill/Irwin   © 2004 The McGraw-Hill Companies

Unearned Revenue - Example 2

After we post the entry to the T-accounts, the
account balances look like this:

Unearned Rent Revenue				Rent Revenue		
12/31	750	12/1	3000		12/31	750
		Bal.	2,250		Bal.	750

McGraw-Hill/Irwin   © 2004 The McGraw-Hill Companies

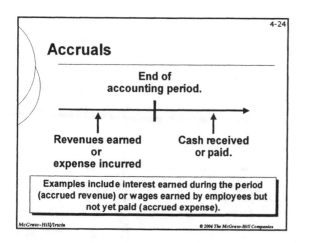

Accrued Revenue - Example 1

On October 1, 2003, Webb, Inc. invests $10,000 for 6 months in a certificate of deposit that pays 6% interest *per year*. Webb will not receive the interest until the CD matures on March 31, 2004. On December 31, 2003, Webb, Inc. must make an entry for the interest earned so far.

GENERAL JOURNAL			Page	352
Date		Description	Debit	Credit
Dec	31	Interest Receivable	150	
		Interest Revenue		150
		$10,000 × 6% × 3/12 = $150		

McGraw-Hill/Irwin © 2004 The McGraw-Hill Companies

Accrued Revenue - Example 1

After we post the entry to the T-accounts, the account balances look like this:

Interest Receivable		Interest Revenue	
12/31 150			12/31 150
Bal. 150			Bal. 150

McGraw-Hill/Irwin © 2004 The McGraw-Hill Companies

Accrued Expenses - Example 2

As of 12/27/03, Denton, Inc. had already paid $1,900,000 in wages for the year. Denton pays its employees every Friday. Year-end, 12/31/03, falls on a Wednesday. The employees have earned total wages of $50,000 for Monday through Wednesday of the week ended 1/02/04.

GENERAL JOURNAL			Page	422
Date		Description	Debit	Credit
Dec	31	Wages Expense	50,000	
		Wages Payable		50,000

McGraw-Hill/Irwin © 2004 The McGraw-Hill Companies

Accrued Expenses - Example 2

After we post the entry to the T-accounts, the account balances look like this:

	Wages Expense		Wages Payable	
As of				
12/27	$1,900,000			12/31 50,000
12/31	50,000			Bal. 50,000
Bal.	$1,950,000			

McGraw-Hill/Irwin © 2004 The McGraw-Hill Companies

Accounting Estimates

- Certain circumstances require adjusting entries to record accounting estimates.
- Examples include . . .
  - Depreciation
  - Bad debts
  - Income taxes

$$$

McGraw-Hill/Irwin © 2004 The McGraw-Hill Companies

Accounting Estimates

- Certain circumstances require adjusting entries to record accounting estimates.
- Examples include . . .
  - Depreciation
  - Bad debts
  - Income taxes

Let's look at how we handle Depreciation expense.

McGraw-Hill/Irwin © 2004 The McGraw-Hill Companies

Depreciation

The accounting concept of *depreciation* involves the *systematic* and *rational* allocation of a long-lived asset's cost to the multiple periods it is used to generate revenue.

This is a "cost allocation" concept, not a "valuation" concept.

Recording Depreciation

The required journal entry requires a debit to *Depreciation expense* and a credit to an account called Accumulated depreciation.

GENERAL JOURNAL			Page	362
Date		Description	Debit	Credit
Dec	31	Depreciation Expense	$$$$	
		Accumulated Depreciation		$$$$

As discussed earlier, this is called a Contra-Asset account.

Depreciation - Example 1

At January 31, 2001, Papa John's trial balance showed Property & equipment of $338,000 (*all numbers in thousands*) and Accumulated depreciation of $83,000. For the period, Papa John's needs to record an additional $2,500 in depreciation.

GENERAL JOURNAL			Page	362
Date		Description	Debit	Credit
Jan	31	Depreciation Expense	2,500	
		Accumulated Depreciation		2,500

Depreciation - Example 1

After we post the entry to the T-accounts, the account balances look like this:

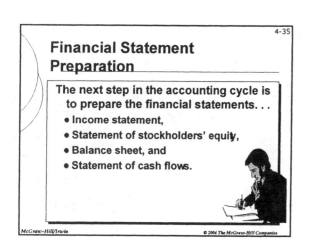

	Depreciation Expense			Accumulated Depreciation	
1/31	2,500			1/31	83,000
				1/31	2,500
Bal.	2,500				
				Bal.	85,500

McGraw-Hill/Irwin   © 2004 The McGraw-Hill Companies

Financial Statement Preparation

The next step in the accounting cycle is to prepare the financial statements. . .

- Income statement,
- Statement of stockholders' equity,
- Balance sheet, and
- Statement of cash flows.

McGraw-Hill/Irwin   © 2004 The McGraw-Hill Companies

Financial Statement Relationships

Net income increases retained earnings, while a net loss will decrease retained earnings. Dividends decrease retained earnings.

DIVIDENDS ——Decrease——▶ RETAINED EARNINGS

Increase ▲

NET INCOME = REVENUES – EXPENSES

McGraw-Hill/Irwin   © 2004 The McGraw-Hill Companies

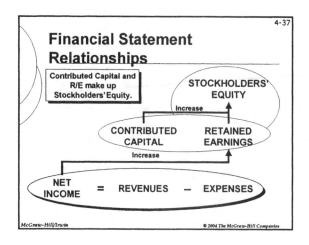

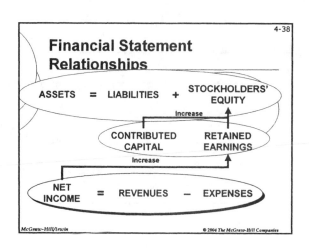

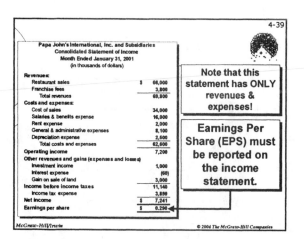

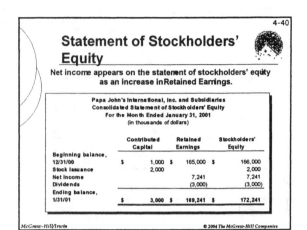

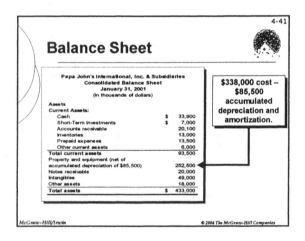

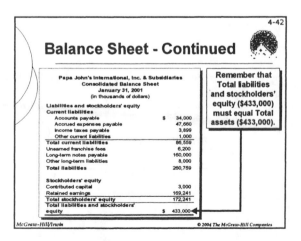

Statement of Cash Flows

4-43

This statement is a categorized list of all transactions of the period that affected the Cash account. The three categories are . . .

1. Operating activities,
2. Investing activities, and
3. Financing activities.

Statement of Cash Flows - General Model

4-44

	Effect on Cash Flows
Operating activities (from Chapter 3)	+/–
Investing activities (from Chapter 2)	+/–
Financing activities (from Chapter 2)	+/–
Changes in cash	Total net cash flows for the period
+ Beginning cash balance	+
= Ending cash balance	Total

Supplemental Disclosure: (1) Interest paid, (2) income taxes paid, and (3) a listing of the nature and amounts of significant noncash transactions.

Key Ratio Analysis: Net Profit Margin

4-45

Net Profit Margin gives an indication of how effective management is at generating profit on every dollar of sales.

$$\text{Net Profit Margin} = \frac{\text{Net income}}{\text{Net sales}}$$

Key Ratio Analysis: Net Profit Margin

The 2000 net profit margin for Papa John's is based on net income of $32,000,000 and on sales of $945,000,000, giving them a net profit margin of 3.39%.

$$\text{Net Profit Margin} = \frac{\text{Net income}}{\text{Net sales}}$$

$$3.39\% = \frac{\$\ 32,000,000}{\$\ 945,000,000}$$

The Closing Process

Even though the balance sheet account balances carry forward from period to period, the income statement accounts do not.

Closing entries:
1. Transfer net income (or loss) to Retained Earnings.
2. Establish a zero balance in each of the *temporary* accounts to start the next accounting period.

The Closing Process

The following accounts are called temporary or nominal accounts and are closed at the end of the period . . .

- Revenues
- Expenses
- Gains,
- Losses, and
- Dividends declared.

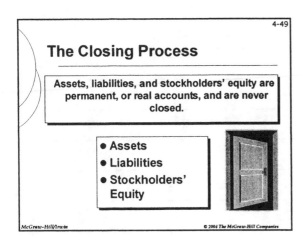

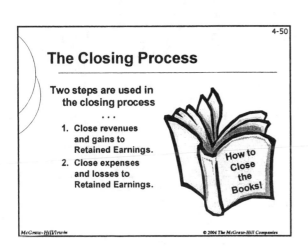

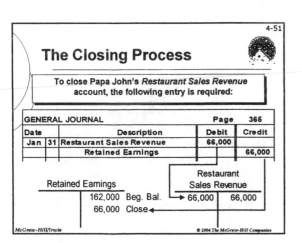

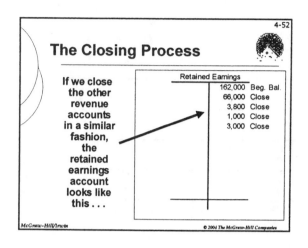

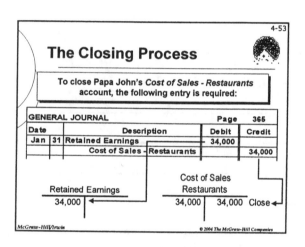

The Closing Process

4-54

If we close the other expense accounts in a similar fashion, the retained earnings account looks like this . . .

Retained Earnings			
Close	34,000	162,000	Beg. Bal.
Close	16,000	66,000	Close
Close	2,000	3,800	Close
Close	8,100	1,000	Close
Close	2,500	3,000	Close
Close	60		
Close	3,899		

McGraw-Hill/Irwin

© 2004 The McGraw-Hill Companies

The Closing Process

Finally, we close dividends to Retained Earnings and the account balances out to $169,241 and looks like this . . .

Retained Earnings			
Close	34,000	162,000	Beg. Bal.
Close	16,000	66,000	Close
Close	2,000	3,800	Close
Close	8,100	1,000	Close
Close	2,500	3,000	Close
Close	60		
Close	3,899		
		169,241	End. Bal

McGraw-Hill/Irwin © 2004 The McGraw-Hill Companies

End of Chapter 4

McGraw-Hill/Irwin © 2004 The McGraw-Hill Companies

Chapter 5

Communicating and
Interpreting
Accounting Information

Players in the
Accounting
Communication
Process

Management
Preparation
CEO, CFO, Accounting Staff
Guided by GAAP

Independent Auditors
Verification
Partners, Managers, Staff
Guided by GAAS

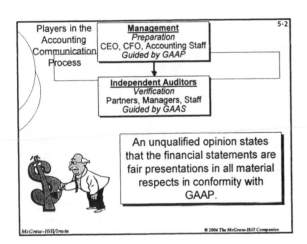

An unqualified opinion states that the financial statements are fair presentations in all material respects in conformity with GAAP.

McGraw-Hill/Irwin   © 2004 The McGraw-Hill Companies

Players in the
Accounting
Communication
Process

Management
Preparation
CFO, CEO, Accounting Staff
Guided by GAAP

Independent Auditors
Verification
Partners, Managers, Staff
Guided by GAAS

Information Intermediaries
Analysis and Advice
Financial analysis,
Information services

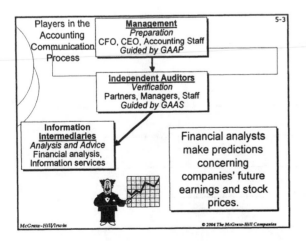

Financial analysts make predictions concerning companies' future earnings and stock prices.

McGraw-Hill/Irwin   © 2004 The McGraw-Hill Companies

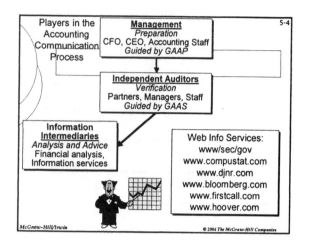

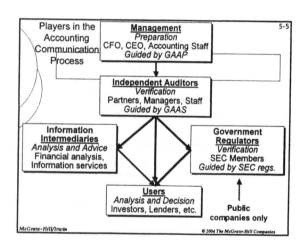

Guiding Principles for Communicating Useful Information

Primary Objective of External Financial Reporting
To provide economic information to external users for decision making.

Primary Qualitative Characteristics
Relevance: Timely and Predictive and Feedback Value
Reliability: Accurate, Unbiased, and Verifiable

Secondary Qualitative Characteristics
Comparability: Across businesses
Consistency: Over time

McGraw-Hill/Irwin   © 2004 The McGraw-Hill Companies

Guiding Principles for Communicating Useful Information

Primary Objective of External Financial Reporting
To provide economic information to external users

The full-disclosure principles requires . . .

1. A complete set of financial statements, and
2. Notes to the financial statements

Secondary Qualitative Characteristics
Comparability: Across businesses
Consistency: Over time

McGraw-Hill/Irwin   © 2004 The McGraw-Hill Companies

The Disclosure Process

Press Releases are used to announce quarterly and annual earnings as soon as the verified figures are available.

Earnings Press Release Excerpt for Gallaway Golf

Callaway® Golf

CARLSBAD, Calif./April 25, 2001/ Gallaway Gold Company (NYSE:ELY) today reported record sales for the first quarter ended March 31, 2001. Reported net sales increased 32% to $261.4 million from $197.4 million during the first quarter of 2000. Net income increased . . . . . .

McGraw-Hill/Irwin   © 2004 The McGraw-Hill Companies

Annual Reports

For privately held companies, annual reports are simple documents that include:

1. Four basic financial statements.
2. Related footnotes.
3. Report of independent accountants (auditor's opinion).

McGraw-Hill/Irwin   © 2004 The McGraw-Hill Companies

Annual Reports

For public companies, annual reports are elaborate because of SEC reporting requirements:

1. *A Nonfinancial Section*

   A letter to the stockholders, a description of management's philosophy, products, successes, etc.

2. *A Financial Section*

   See next slide for a detailed listing . . .

Annual Reports - Financial Section

1. Summarized financial data for 5- or 10-years.
2. Management Discussion and Analysis (MD&A).
3. The four basic financial statements.
4. Notes (footnotes).
5. Independent Accountant's Report.

6. Recent stock price information.
7. Summaries of the unaudited quarterly financial data.
8. Lists of directors and officers of the company and relevant addresses.

Quarterly Reports

Usually begin with short letter to stockholders,

✓Condensed *unaudited* income statement and balance sheet for the quarter.

✓Often, cash flow statement and statement of stockholders' equity are *omitted*. Some notes to the financial statements also may be omitted.

SEC Reports

Form 10-K Annual Report
- Due within 90 days of the fiscal year-end
- Contains audited financial statements

Form 10-Q Quarterly Report
- Due within 45 days of the end of the quarter
- Financial statements can be unaudited

Form 8-K Current Report
- Due within 15 days of the major event date
- Financial statements can be unaudited

McGraw-Hill/Irwin   © 2004 The McGraw-Hill Companies

Financial Statement Formats

Let's take a closer look at the asset section of the balance sheet!

McGraw-Hill/Irwin   © 2004 The McGraw-Hill Companies

Consolidated Balance Sheet

(in thousands, except share data and per share data)	December 31, 2000	1999
ASSETS		
Current assets:		
Cash and cash equivalents	$ 102,596	$ 112,602
Accounts receivable, net	58,836	54,252
Inventories, net	133,962	97,938
Deferred taxes	29,354	32,558
Other current assets	17,721	13,122
Total current assets	342,469	310,472
Property, plant and equipment, net	134,712	142,214
Intangible assets, net	112,824	120,143
Other assets	40,929	43,954
	$ 630,934	$ 616,783

McGraw-Hill/Irwin   © 2004 The McGraw-Hill Companies

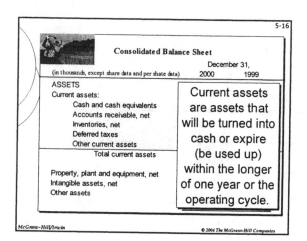

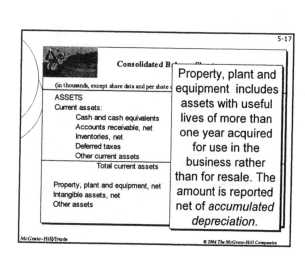

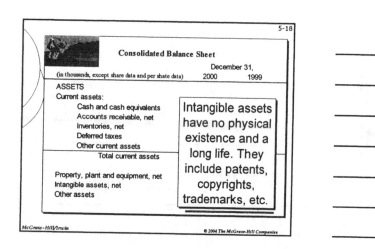

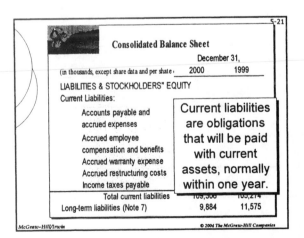

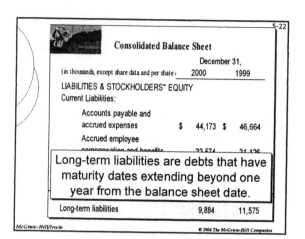

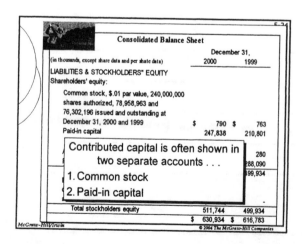

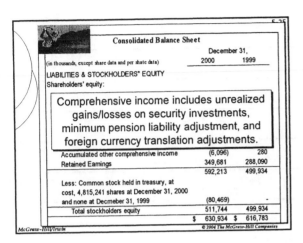

Consolidated Balance Sheet

(in thousands, except share data and per share data)	December 31,	
	2000	1999

LIABILITIES & STOCKHOLDERS" EQUITY
Shareholders' equity:

> Comprehensive income includes unrealized gains/losses on security investments, minimum pension liability adjustment, and foreign currency translation adjustments.

Accumulated other comprehensive income	(6,096)	280
Retained Earnings	349,681	288,090
	592,213	499,934
Less: Common stock held in treasury, at cost, 4,815,241 shares at December 31, 2000 and none at Decmeber 31, 1999	(80,469)	-
Total stockholders equity	511,744	499,934
	$ 630,934	$ 616,783

McGraw-Hill/Irwin   © 2004 The McGraw-Hill Companies

Consolidated Balance Sheet

(in thousands, except share data and per share data)	December 31,	
	2000	1999

LIABILITIES & STOCKHOLDERS" EQUITY
Shareholders' equity:

> Retained earnings is the total earnings of the company less the total dividends declared since inception of operations.

Retained Earnings	349,681	288,090
	592,213	499,934
Less: Common stock held in treasury, at cost, 4,815,241 shares at December 31, 2000 and none at Decmeber 31, 1999	(80,469)	-
Total stockholders equity	511,744	499,934
	$ 630,934	$ 616,783

McGraw-Hill/Irwin   © 2004 The McGraw-Hill Companies

Consolidated Balance Sheet

(in thousands, except share data and per share data)	December 31,	
	2000	1999

LIABILITIES & STOCKHOLDERS" EQUITY
Shareholders' equity:

Common stock, $.01 par value, 240,000,000 shares authorized, 78,958,963 and

> Companies often purchase share s of its own common stock. This stock is said to be held in the treasury and can be used to satisfy employee stock purchase or option plans. Treasury shares may also be used in connection with the acquisition of another company.

Less: Common stock held in treasury, at cost, 4,815,241 shares at December 31, 2000 and none at Decmeber 31, 1999	(80,469)	-
Total stockholders equity	511,744	499,934
	$ 630,934	$ 616,783

McGraw-Hill/Irwin   © 2004 The McGraw-Hill Companies

5-28

Balance Sheet Ratios and Debt Contracts

When a company borrows money, they often agree to certain restrictions on their activity. Ratios typically part of the borrowing agreement include:

Total Liabilities
÷ **Stockholders' Equity**
= **Debt-to-Equity Ratio**

Current Assets
÷ **Current Liabilities**
= **Current Ratio**

McGraw-Hill/Irwin   © 2004 The McGraw-Hill Companies

5-29

Classified Income Statement

Income statements may contain five sections:

1. Continuing operations
2. Discontinued operations
3. Extraordinary items
4. Cumulative effect of changes in accounting methods
5. Earnings per share

McGraw-Hill/Irwin   © 2004 The McGraw-Hill Companies

5-30

Classified Income Statement

General Format for the Classified Income Statement

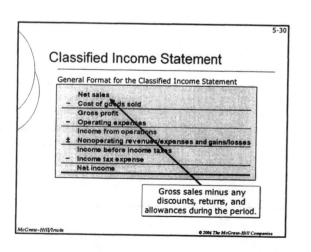

Net sales
− Cost of goods sold
  Gross profit
− Operating expenses
  Income from operations
± Nonoperating revenues/expenses and gains/losses
  Income before income taxes
− Income tax expense
  Net income

Gross sales minus any discounts, returns, and allowances during the period.

McGraw-Hill/Irwin   © 2004 The McGraw-Hill Companies

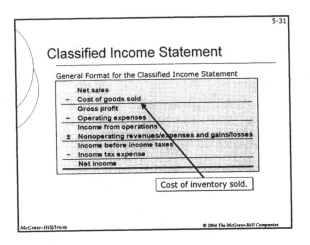

Classified Income Statement

General Format for the Classified Income Statement

	Net sales
−	Cost of goods sold
	Gross profit
−	Operating expenses
	Income from operations
±	Nonoperating revenues/expenses and gains/losses
	Income before income taxes
−	Income tax expense
	Net income

Cost of inventory sold.

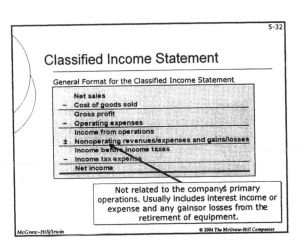

Classified Income Statement

General Format for the Classified Income Statement

	Net sales
−	Cost of goods sold
	Gross profit
−	Operating expenses
	Income from operations
±	Nonoperating revenues/expenses and gains/losses
	Income before income taxes
−	Income tax expense
	Net income

Not related to the company's primary operations. Usually includes interest income or expense and any gains or losses from the retirement of equipment.

Classified Income Statement

In addition, companies may have nonrecurring items. These nonrecurring items may include:

1. Discontinued operations,
2. Extraordinary items,
3. Cumulative effect of changes in accounting methods.

These items are reported separately because they are not useful in predicting future income of the company.

Net income

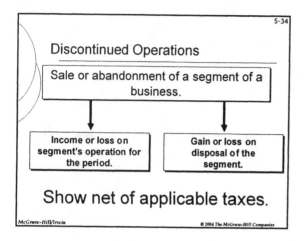

Discontinued Operations

Sale or abandonment of a segment of a business.

Income or loss on segment's operation for the period.

Gain or loss on disposal of the segment.

Show net of applicable taxes.

McGraw-Hill/Irwin   © 2004 The McGraw-Hill Companies

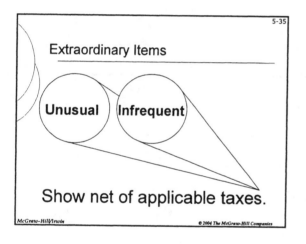

Extraordinary Items

Unusual   Infrequent

Show net of applicable taxes.

McGraw-Hill/Irwin   © 2004 The McGraw-Hill Companies

Cumulative Effect of Changes in Accounting Methods

GAAP Method — Change to Alternative → **GAAP Method**

The change must be to a *preferable method* and must be disclosed in notes to financial statements.

Show net of applicable taxes.

McGraw-Hill/Irwin   © 2004 The McGraw-Hill Companies

Classified Income Statement

Now, let's look at two common formats for presenting the continuing operations section.

1. Single-step income statement
2. Multiple-step income statement

McGraw-Hill/Irwin · © 2004 The McGraw-Hill Companies

Single Step

(in thousands)

	2000
Net sales	$ 837,627
Interest income and other income, net	7,267
Total revenues	844,894
Cost of goods sold	440,119
Selling expenses	170,541
General & Administrative expenses	70,333
Research and development costs	34,579
Other items	957
Total expenses	716,529
Income before income taxes	128,365
Provision for income taxes	47,366
Net income	$ 80,999

In the *single-step* format, all revenues, income, and gains are listed first.

Costs, expenses, and losses are then subtracted from total revenues to get net income.

McGraw-Hill/Irwin · © 2004 The McGraw-Hill Companies

Multiple Step

(in thousands)

	2000
Net sales	$ 837,627
Cost of goods sold	440,119
Gross Profit	397,508
Selling expenses	170,541
General & Administrative expenses	70,333
Research and development costs	34,579
Income from Operations	122,055
Interest income and other income, net	7,267
Income before income taxes	129,322
Provision for income taxes	47,366
Income before cumulative effect	81,956
Cumulative effect of accounting change	(957)
Net income	$ 80,999

Cost of goods sold is shown along with a separation of non-operating income and expenses and non-recurring items.

McGraw-Hill/Irwin · © 2004 The McGraw-Hill Companies

Slide 1

Consolidated Statement of Income
(in thousands, except per share data)

	2000		1999	
Net sales	$ 837,627	100%	$ 719,038	100%
Cost of goods sold	440,119	53%	384,265	53%
Gross profit	397,508	47%	334,773	47%
Selling expenses	170,541	20%	128,565	18%
General & Admin. expenses	70,333	8%	92,478	13%
Research and development costs	34,579	4%	34,002	5%
Restructuring costs	-		(5,894)	-1%
Sumitomo transition costs	-		5,713	1%
Income from operations	122,055	15%	79,909	11%
Interest and other income, net	8,791		9,182	
Interest expense	(1,524)		(3,594)	
Income before income taxes	129,322	16%	85,497	12%
Provision for income taxes	47,366		30,175	
Cumulative effect of accounting change	(957)		-	
Net income	$ 80,999	10%	$ 55,322	8%
Earnings per common share				
Basic				
Income before accounting change	$ 1.17		$ 0.79	
Cumulative effect of change	(0.01)			
	$ 1.16		$ 0.79	
Diluted				
Income before accounting change	$ 1.14		$ 0.78	
Cumulative effect of change	(0.01)			
	$ 1.13		$ 0.78	
Common equivalent shares				
Basic	69,946		70,397	
Diluted	71,412		71,214	

Two unusual expenses that may recur in the future.

McGraw-Hill/Irwin

Slide 2

Consolidated Statement of Income
(in thousands, except per share data)

	2000		1999	
Net sales	$ 837,627	100%	$ 719,038	100%
Cost of goods sold	440,119	53%	384,265	53%
Gross profit	397,508	47%	334,773	47%
Selling expenses	170,541	20%	128,565	18%
General & Admin. expenses	70,333	8%	92,478	13%
Research and development costs	34,579	4%	34,002	5%
Restructuring costs	-		(5,894)	-1%
Sumitomo transition costs	-		5,713	1%
Income from operations	122,055	15%	79,909	11%
Interest and other income, net	8,791		9,182	
Interest expense	(1,524)		(3,594)	
Income before income taxes	129,322	16%	85,497	12%
Provision for income taxes	47,366		30,175	
Cumulative effect of accounting change	(957)		-	
Net income	$ 80,999	10%	$ 55,322	8%
Earnings per common share				
Basic				
Income before accounting change	$ 1.17		$ 0.79	
Cumulative effect of change	(0.01)			
	$ 1.16		$ 0.79	
Diluted				
Income before accounting change	$ 1.14		$ 0.78	
Cumulative effect of change	(0.01)			
	$ 1.13		$ 0.78	
Common equivalent shares				
Basic	69,946		70,397	
Diluted	71,412		71,214	

A nonrecurring item that is presented separately after income from operations.

McGraw-Hill/Irwin

Slide 3

Earnings Per Share

$$EPS = \frac{\text{Net Income Available to Common Shareholders}}{\text{Weighted Average Number of Shares Outstanding During the Reporting Period}}$$

Basic EPS

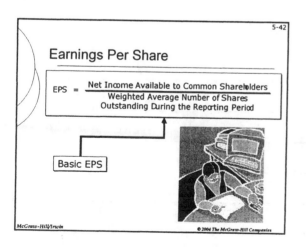

McGraw-Hill/Irwin

© 2004 The McGraw-Hill Companies

Earnings Per Share

$$EPS = \frac{\text{Net Income Available to Common Shareholders}}{\text{Weighted Average Number of Shares Outstanding During the Reporting Period}}$$

Diluted EPS
Stock options, debt securities, equity securities are assumed to be converted into common stock at the beginning of the period.

McGraw-Hill/Irwin   © 2004 The McGraw-Hill Companies

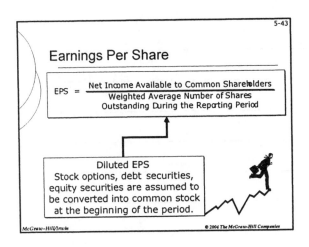

Consolidated Statement of Income
(In thousands, except per share data)

	2000		1999	
Net sales	$ 837,627	100%	$ 719,038	100%
Cost of goods sold	440,119	53%	364,265	53%
Gross profit	397,508	47%	334,773	47%
Selling expenses	170,541	20%	128,565	18%
General & Admin. expenses	70,333	8%	92,478	13%
Research and development costs	34,579	4%	34,002	5%
Restructuring costs	-		(5,894)	-1%
Sumitomo transition costs	-		5,713	1%
Income from operations	122,055	15%	79,909	11%
Interest and other income, net	8,791		9,182	
Interest expense	(1,524)		(3,594)	
Income before income taxes	129,322	16%	85,497	12%
Provision for income taxes	47,366		30,175	
Cumulative effect of accounting change	(957)		-	
Net income	$ 80,999	10%	$ 55,322	8%
Earnings per common share				
Basic				
Income before accounting change	$ 1.17		$ 0.79	
Cumulative effect of change	(0.01)			
	$ 1.16		$ 0.79	
Diluted				
Income before accounting change	$ 1.14		$ 0.78	
Cumulative effect of change	(0.01)			
	$ 1.13		$ 0.78	
Common equivalent shares				
Basic	69,946		70,397	
Diluted	71,412		71,214	

Both basic and diluted EPS are reported here.

McGraw-Hill/Irwin

Accounting-Based Executive Bonuses

Executives are frequently paid bonuses based upon pretax earnings growth of the company.

$$\text{Pre-Tax Earnings Growth Percent} = \frac{\left(\begin{array}{c}\text{Current Year}\\ \text{Pretax Earnings}\end{array}\right) - \left(\begin{array}{c}\text{Last Year}\\ \text{Pretax Earnings}\end{array}\right)}{\text{Last Year Pretax Earnings}}$$

McGraw-Hill/Irwin   © 2004 The McGraw-Hill Companies

Statement of Cash Flows

Recall that the Statement of Cash Flows is divided into *three* major sections.

1. Cash flows from operating activities.
2. Cash flows from investing activities.
3. Cash flows from financing activities.

We will examine the indirect method of preparing the statement. This format begins with a *reconciliation* of accrual income to cash flows from operations.

McGraw-Hill/Irwin
© 2004 The McGraw-Hill Companies

The operating activities section of Callaway using the *indirect method*. Begin with accounting net income and arrive at cash provided by operating activities.

Consolidated Statement of Cash Flows
(in thousands)

	2000
Cash flows from operating activities:	
Net income	$ 80,999
Adjustments to reconcile net income to net cash provided by operating activities:	
Depreciation & amortization	40,249
Non-cash compensation	2,157
Tax benefit from exercise of stock options	6,806
Net non-cash foreign currency gains	(1,410)
Deferred taxes	4,906
Loss on disposal of assets	342
Increase (decrease) in cash resulting from changes in:	
Accounts receivable, net	(9,047)
Inventories, net	(39,402)
Other assets	(3,074)
Accounts payable and accrued expenses	2,638
Accrued employee compensation and benefits	1,623
Accrued warranty expense	3,258
Income taxes payable	4,088
Accrued restructuring costs	(1,379)
Deferred compensation	(1,691)
Net cash provided by operating activities	91,063

McGraw-Hill/Irwin

While these items are on the income statement, they have no current cash effect.

Consolidated Statement of Cash Flows
(in thousands)

	2000
Cash flows from operating activities:	
Net income	$ 80,999
Adjustments to reconcile net income to net cash provided by operating activities:	
Depreciation & amortization	40,249
Non-cash compensation	2,157
Tax benefit from exercise of stock options	6,806
Net non-cash foreign currency gains	(1,410)
Deferred taxes	4,906
Loss on disposal of assets	342
Increase (decrease) in cash resulting from changes in:	
Accounts receivable, net	(9,047)
Inventories, net	(39,402)
Other assets	(3,074)
Accounts payable and accrued expenses	2,638
Accrued employee compensation and benefits	1,623
Accrued warranty expense	3,258
Income taxes payable	4,088
Accrued restructuring costs	(1,379)
Deferred compensation	(1,691)
Net cash provided by operating activities	91,063

McGraw-Hill/Irwin

Consolidated Statement of Cash Flows
(in thousands)

	2000
Cash flows from operating activities:	
Net income	$ 80,999

Change in Account Balance During Year		
	Increase	**Decrease**
Current Assets	Subtract from net income.	Add to net income.
Current Liabilities	Add to net income.	Subtract from net income.

changes in:	
Accounts receivable, net	(9,047)
Inventories, net	(39,402)
Other assets	(3,074)
Accounts payable and accrued expenses	2,638
Accrued employee compensation and benefits	1,623
Accrued warranty expense	3,258
Income taxes payable	4,088
Accrued restructuring costs	(1,379)
Deferred compensation	(1,691)
Net cash provided by operating activities	91,063

This table provides guidance for adjustments related to changes in current assets and current liabilities.

McGraw-Hill/Irwin

Consolidated Statement of Cash Flows
(in thousands)

	2000
Cash flows from investing activities	
Capital expenditures	$ (28,386)
Acquisition, net of cash acquired	(444)
Proceeds from sale of assets	244
Net cash used in investing activities	(28,586)
Cash flows from financing activities:	
Issuance of common stock	28,233
Acquisition of treasury stock	(80,469)
Proceeds from sale-leaseback of equipment	1,268
Dividends paid, net	(19,538)
Net cash used in financing activities	(70,506)
Effect of exchange rate changes on cash	(1,977)
Net (decrease) increase in cash and cash equivalents	(10,006)
Cash and cash equivalents at beginning of year	112,602
Cash and cash equivalents at end of year	$ 102,596
Supplemental disclosure:	
Cash paid for interest and fees	$ 805
Cash paid for income taxes	29,245

Here is the rest of Callaway's Statement of Cash Flows showing the cash balance on the company's balance sheet.

McGraw-Hill/Irwin   © 2004 The McGraw-Hill Companies

Notes to Financial Statements

Descriptions of the key accounting rules applies to the company's statements.

Additional detail supporting reported numbers.

Relevant financial information not disclosed on the statements.

McGraw-Hill/Irwin   © 2004 The McGraw-Hill Companies

Return on Equity (ROE)

5-52

$$\text{Return on Equity} = \frac{\text{Net Income}}{\text{Average Stockholder's Equity}^1}$$

ROE measures how much the firm earned for each dollar of stockholders' investment.

^{1}(beginning equity + ending equity) ÷ 2

McGraw-Hill/Irwin   © 2004 The McGraw-Hill Companies

ROE Profit Driver Analysis

5-53

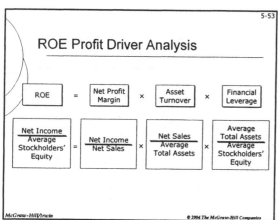

ROE = Net Profit Margin × Asset Turnover × Financial Leverage

$$\frac{\text{Net Income}}{\text{Average Stockholders' Equity}} = \frac{\text{Net Income}}{\text{Net Sales}} \times \frac{\text{Net Sales}}{\text{Average Total Assets}} \times \frac{\text{Average Total Assets}}{\text{Average Stockholders' Equity}}$$

McGraw-Hill/Irwin   © 2004 The McGraw-Hill Companies

Profit Drivers and Business Strategy

5-54

High-value or product-differentiation.
Rely on R&D and product promotion to convince customers of the superiority of their product.

Low-Cost.
Rely on efficient management of account receivable, inventory and productive assets to product high asset turnover.

McGraw-Hill/Irwin   © 2004 The McGraw-Hill Companies

The End of Chapter 5

Chapter 6

Reporting and Interpreting Sales Revenue, Receivables, and Cash

---

Accounting for Sales Revenue

The revenue principle requires that revenues be recorded when earned:

An exchange has taken place.

The earnings process is nearly complete.

Collection is probable.

McGraw-Hill/Irwin   © 2004 The McGraw-Hill Companies

Reporting Net Sales

Companies record sales discounts, sales returns and allowances, and credit card discounts separately to allow management to monitor these transactions.

Sales revenue
Less: Sales returns and allowances
            Sales discounts
            Credit card discounts
Net sales

McGraw-Hill/Irwin   © 2004 The McGraw-Hill Companies

Credit Card Sales to Consumers

Companies accept credit cards for several reasons:

1. To increase sales.

2. To avoid providing credit directly to customers.

3. To avoid losses due to bad checks.

4. To receive payment quicker.

McGraw-Hill/Irwin © 2004 The McGraw-Hill Companies

Credit Card Sales to Consumers

When credit card sales are made, the company must pay the credit card company a fee for the service it provides.

McGraw-Hill/Irwin © 2004 The McGraw-Hill Companies

Credit Card Sales to Consumers

On January 2, a Timberland factory store's credit card sales were $3,000. The credit card company charges a 3% service fee.

Prepare the Timberland journal entry.

GENERAL JOURNAL			Page 34
Date	Description	Debit	Credit
Jan. 2			

McGraw-Hill/Irwin © 2004 The McGraw-Hill Companies

Credit Card Sales to Consumers

On January 2, a Timberland factory store's credit card sales were $3,000. The credit card company charges a 3% service fee.

> Credit Card Discounts are reported as a contra revenue account.

GENERAL JOURNAL			Page 34	
Date		Description	Debit	Credit
Jan.	2	Accounts Receivable	2,910	
		Credit Card Discounts	90	
		Sales Revenue		3,000
		$3,000 × 3% = $90 Credit Card Fee		

McGraw-Hill/Irwin   © 2004 The McGraw-Hill Companies

Sales to Businesses on Account

When companies allow customers to purchase merchandise on an open account, the customer promises to pay the company in the future for the purchase.

Fontana Shoes

McGraw-Hill/Irwin   © 2004 The McGraw-Hill Companies

Sales Discounts to Businesses

2/10, n/30

Read as: "Two ten, net thirty"

When customers purchase on open account, they may be offered a sales discount to encourage early payment.

McGraw-Hill/Irwin   © 2004 The McGraw-Hill Companies

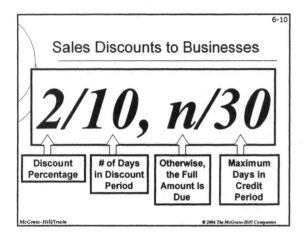

Sales Discounts to Businesses

2/10, n/30

| Discount Percentage | # of Days in Discount Period | Otherwise, the Full Amount Is Due | Maximum Days in Credit Period |

McGraw-Hill/Irwin © 2004 The McGraw-Hill Companies

Sales Discounts to Businesses

On January 6, Timberland sold $1,000 of merchandise on credit with terms of 2/10, n/30. Prepare the Timberland journal entry.

| **GENERAL JOURNAL** | | | Page 34 |
Date	Description	Debit	Credit
Jan. 6			

McGraw-Hill/Irwin © 2004 The McGraw-Hill Companies

Sales Discounts to Businesses

On January 6, Timberland sold $1,000 of merchandise on credit with terms of 2/10, n/30. Prepare the Timberland journal entry.

| **GENERAL JOURNAL** | | | Page 34 |
Date	Description	Debit	Credit
Jan. 6	Accounts Receivable	1,000	
	Sales Revenue		1,000

McGraw-Hill/Irwin © 2004 The McGraw-Hill Companies

Sales Discounts to Businesses

On January 14, Timberland receives the appropriate payment from the customer for the January 6 sale.

Prepare the Timberland journal entry.

GENERAL JOURNAL			Page 34	
Date	**Description**		**Debit**	**Credit**
Jan. 14				

McGraw-Hill/Irwin   © 2004 The McGraw-Hill Companies

Sales Discounts to Businesses

On January 14, Timberland receives the appropriate payment from the customer for the January 6 sale.

Prepare the Timberland journal entry.

	$1,000 × 2% = $20 sales discount		Page 34	
Date	$1,000 - $20 = $980 cash receipt			**Credit**
Jan. 14	Cash		980	
	Sales Discounts		20	
	Accounts Receivable			1,000

McGraw-Hill/Irwin   Contra-revenue account   © 2004 The McGraw-Hill Companies

Sales Discounts to Businesses

If the customer remits the appropriate amount on January 20 instead of January 14, what entry would Timberland make?

GENERAL JOURNAL			Page 34	
Date	**Description**		**Debit**	**Credit**
Jan. 20				

McGraw-Hill/Irwin   © 2004 The McGraw-Hill Companies

Sales Discounts to Businesses

If the customer remits the appropriate amount on January 20 instead of January 14, what entry would Timberland make?

Since the customer paid outside of the discount period, a sales discount is not granted.

Date		Description	Debit	Credit
Jan.	20	Cash	1,000	
		Accounts Receivable		1,000

To Take or Not Take the Discount

With discount terms of 2/10,n/30, a customer saves $2 on a $100 purchase by paying on the 10th day instead of the 30th day.

$$\text{Interest Rate for 20 Days} = \frac{\text{Amount Saved}}{\text{Amount Paid}}$$

$$\text{Interest Rate for 20 Days} = \frac{\$2}{\$98} = 2.04\%$$

$$\text{Annual Interest Rate} = \frac{365 \text{ Days}}{20 \text{ Days}} \times 2.04\% = 37.23\%$$

Sales Returns and Allowances

Debited for damaged merchandise.

Debited for returned merchandise.

Contra revenue account.

Sales Returns and Allowances

On July 8, Fontana Shoes returns $500 of hiking boots originally purchased on account from Timberland.

Prepare the Timberland journal entry.

GENERAL JOURNAL			Page 40	
Date	Description		Debit	Credit
July 8				

Sales Returns and Allowances

On July 8, Fontana Shoes returns $500 of hiking boots originally purchased on account from Timberland.

Prepare the Timberland journal entry.

GENERAL JOURNAL			Page 40	
Date	Description		Debit	Credit
July 8	Sales Returns and Allowances		500	
	Accounts Receivable			500

Gross Profit Percentage

$$\text{Gross Profit Percentage} = \frac{\text{Gross Profit}}{\text{Net Sales}}$$

In 2000, Timberland reported gross profit of $508,512,000 on sales of $1,091,478,000.

All other things equal, a higher gross profit results in higher net income.

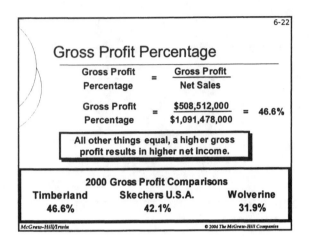

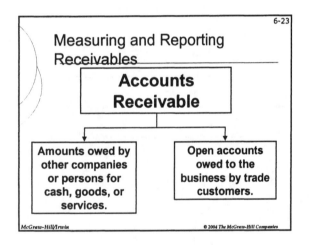

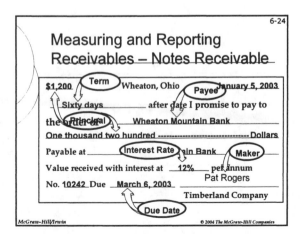

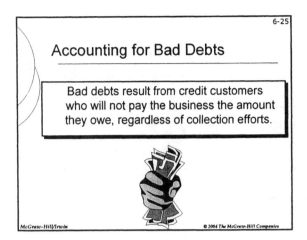

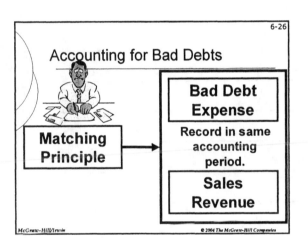

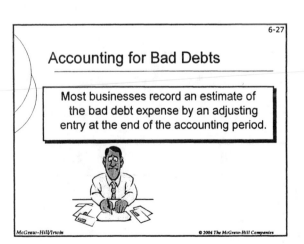

Recording Bad Debt Expense Estimates

Timberland estimated bad debt expense for 2000 to be $2,395,000.

Prepare the adjusting entry.

GENERAL JOURNAL			Page 78
Date	Description	Debit	Credit
Dec. 31			

McGraw-Hill/Irwin   © 2004 The McGraw-Hill Companies

Recording Bad Debt Expense Estimates

Timberland estimated bad debt expense for 2000 to be $2,395,000.

Prepare the adjusting entry.

Bad Debt Expense is normally classified as a selling expense and is closed at year-end.		Page 78	
Date			Credit
Dec. 31	Bad Debt Expense	2,395,000	
	Allowance for Doubtful Accounts		2,395,000

Contra asset account

McGraw-Hill/Irwin   © 2004 The McGraw-Hill Companies

Allowance for Doubtful Accounts

Balance Sheet Disclosure

Accounts receivable
Less: Allowance for doubtful accounts
Net realizable value of accounts receivable

Amount the business expects to collect.

McGraw-Hill/Irwin   © 2004 The McGraw-Hill Companies

Writing Off Uncollectible Accounts

When it is clear that a specific customer's account receivable will be uncollectible, the amount should be removed from the Accounts Receivable account and charged to the Allowance for Doubtful Accounts.

McGraw-Hill/Irwin © 2004 The McGraw-Hill Companies

Writing Off Uncollectible Accounts

Timberland's total write-offs for 2000 were $1,480,000.
Prepare a summary journal entry for these write-offs.

	GENERAL JOURNAL		Page 37
Date	Description	Debit	Credit

McGraw-Hill/Irwin © 2004 The McGraw-Hill Companies

Writing Off Uncollectible Accounts

Timberland's total write-offs for 2000 were $1,480,000.
Prepare a summary journal entry for these write-offs.

	GENERAL JOURNAL		Page 37
Date	Description	Debit	Credit
	Allowance for Doubtful Accounts	1,480,000	
	Accounts Receivable		1,480,000

McGraw-Hill/Irwin © 2004 The McGraw-Hill Companies

Writing Off Uncollectible Accounts

Assume that before the write-off, Timberland's Accounts Receivable balance was $81,000,000 and the Allowance for Doubtful Accounts balance was $2,000,000.

Let's see what effect the total write-offs of $1,480,000 had on these accounts.

McGraw-Hill/Irwin   © 2004 The McGraw-Hill Companies

Writing Off Uncollectible Accounts

	Before Write-Off	After Write-Off
Accounts receivable	$ 81,000,000	$ 79,520,000
Less: Allow. for doubtful accts.	2,000,000	520,000
Net realizable value	$ 79,000,000	$ 79,000,000

Notice that the total write-offs of $1,480,000 did not change the net realizable value nor did it affect any income statement accounts.

McGraw-Hill/Irwin   © 2004 The McGraw-Hill Companies

Methods for Estimating Bad Debts

Percentage of credit sales
or
Aging of accounts receivable

McGraw-Hill/Irwin   © 2004 The McGraw-Hill Companies

Percentage of Credit Sales

Bad debt percentage is based on actual uncollectible accounts from prior years' credit sales.

Focus is on determining the amount to record on the income statement as Bad Debt Expense.

Percentage of Credit Sales

Net Credit Sales
× % Estimated Uncollectible
Amount of Journal Entry

Percentage of Credit Sales

In 2003, Kid's Clothes had credit sales of $60,000. Past experience indicates that bad debts are one percent of sales.

What is the estimate of bad debts expense for 2003?

Percentage of Credit Sales

In 2003, Kid's Clothes had credit sales of $60,000. Past experience indicates that bad debts are one percent of sales.

What is the estimate of bad debts expense for 2003?

$60,000 × .01 = $600

Now, prepare the adjusting entry.

McGraw-Hill/Irwin   © 2004 The McGraw-Hill Companies

Percentage of Credit Sales

GENERAL JOURNAL		Page 76	
Date	Description	Debit	Credit
Dec. 31	Bad Debt Expense	600	
	Allowance for Doubtful Accounts		600

McGraw-Hill/Irwin   © 2004 The McGraw-Hill Companies

Now let's discuss another method that is used to account for uncollectible accounts.

McGraw-Hill/Irwin   © 2004 The McGraw-Hill Companies

Aging of Accounts Receivable

Focus is on determining the desired balance in the Allowance for Doubtful Accounts on the balance sheet.

McGraw-Hill/Irwin   © 2004 The McGraw-Hill Companies

Aging of Accounts Receivable

   Accounts Receivable
× **% Estimated Uncollectible**
   Desired Balance in Allowance Account
- **Allowance Account Credit Balance**
   Amount of Journal Entry

   Accounts Receivable
× **% Estimated Uncollectible**
   Desired Balance in Allowance Account
+ **Allowance Account Debit Balance**
   Amount of Journal Entry

McGraw-Hill/Irwin   © 2004 The McGraw-Hill Companies

Aging Schedule

Each customer's account is aged by breaking down the balance by showing the age (in number of days) of each part of the balance.

An aging of accounts receivable for Kid's Clothes in 2003 might look like this . . .

McGraw-Hill/Irwin   © 2004 The McGraw-Hill Companies

Slide 6-46

Aging Schedule

| Customer | Not Yet Due | Days Past Due | | | | Total A/R Balance |
		1-30	31-60	61-90	Over 90	
Aaron, R.		$ 235				$ 235
Baxter, T.	$1,200	300				1,500
Clark, J.			$ 50	$ 200	$ 500	750
Zak, R.			325			325
Total	$3,500	$2,550	$1,830	$1,540	$1,240	$10,660

Based on past experience, the business estimates the percentage of uncollectible accounts in each time category.

Slide 6-47

Aging Schedule

| Customer | Not Yet Due | Days Past Due | | | | Total A/R Balance |
		1-30	31-60	61-90	Over 90	
Aaron, R.		$ 235				$ 235
Baxter, T.	$1,200	300				1,500
Clark, J.			$ 50	$ 200	$ 500	750
Zak, R.			325			325
Total	$3,500	$2,550	$1,830	$1,540	$1,240	$10,660
% Uncollectible	0.01	0.04	0.10	0.25	0.40	

These percentages are then multiplied by the appropriate column totals.

Slide 6-48

Aging Schedule

| Customer | Not Yet Due | Days Past Due | | | | Total A/R Balance |
		1-30	31-60	61-90	Over 90	
Aaron, R.						235
Baxter, T.	$1,200	300				1,500
Clark, J.			$ 50	$ 200	$ 500	750
Zak, R.			325			325
Total	$3,500	$2,550	$1,830	$1,540	$1,240	$10,660
% Uncollectible	0.01	0.04	0.10	0.25	0.40	
Estimated Uncoll. Amount	$ 35	$ 102	$ 183	$ 385	$ 496	$ 1,201

The column totals are then added to arrive at the total estimate of uncollectible accounts of $1,201.

Slide 6-49

Aging of Accounts Receivable

	Days Past Due					
Customer						tal R nce
Aaron, R.		Record the Dec. 31, 2003, adjusting				235
Baxter, T.		entry assuming that the Allowance				500
Clark, J.		for Doubtful Accounts currently has				750
		a $50 credit balance.				
Zak, R.			325			325
Total	$3,500	$2,550	$1,830	$1,540	$1,240	$10,660
% Uncollectible	0.01	0.04	0.10	0.25	0.40	
Estimated Uncoll. Amount	$ 35	$ 102	$ 183	$ 385	$ 496	$ 1,201

McGraw-Hill/Irwin   © 2004 The McGraw-Hill Companies

Slide 6-50

Aging of Accounts Receivable

	GENERAL JOURNAL			Page 76
Date	Description	Post. Ref.	Debit	Credit
Dec. 31	Bad Debt Expense		1,151	
	Allowance for Doubtful Accounts			1,151

	1,201	Desired Balance
-	50	Credit Balance
	$ 1,151	Adjusting Entry

After posting, the Allowance account would look like this . . .

McGraw-Hill/Irwin   © 2004 The McGraw-Hill Companies

Slide 6-51

Aging of Accounts Receivable

Allowance for Doubtful Accounts

	50	Balance at 12/31/2003 before adj.
	1,151	2003 adjustment
	1,201	Balance at 12/31/2003 after adj.

Notice that the balance after adjustment is equal to the estimate of $1,201 based on the aging analysis performed earlier.

McGraw-Hill/Irwin   © 2004 The McGraw-Hill Companies

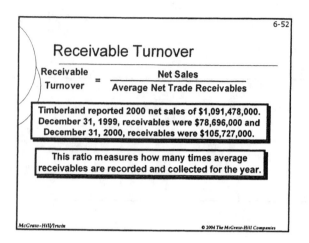

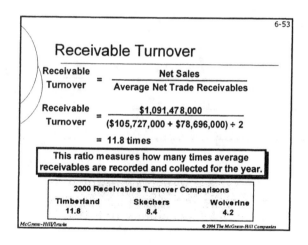

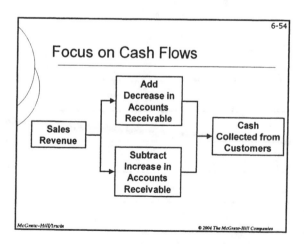

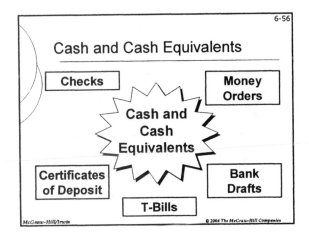

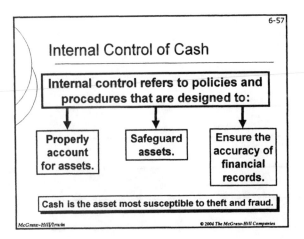

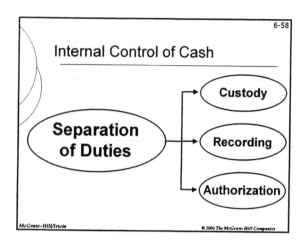

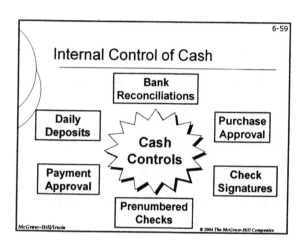

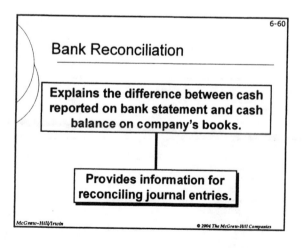

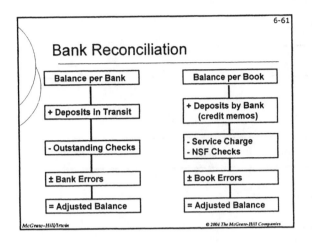

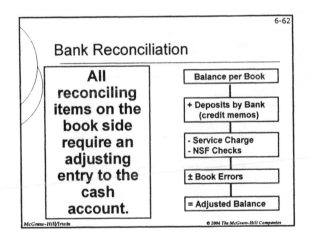

6-63

Bank Reconciliation

Prepare a July 31 bank reconciliation statement and the resulting journal entries for the Simmons Company. The July 31 bank statement indicated a cash balance of $9,610, while the cash ledger account on that date shows a balance of $7,430.

Additional information necessary for the reconciliation is shown on the next page.

McGraw-Hill/Irwin   © 2004 The McGraw-Hill Companies

Bank Reconciliation

- Outstanding checks totaled $2,417.
- A $500 check mailed to the bank for deposit had not reached the bank at the statement date.
- The bank returned a customer's NSF check for $225 received as payment of an account receivable.
- The bank statement showed $30 interest earned on the bank balance for the month of July.
- Check 781 for supplies cleared the bank for $268 but was erroneously recorded in our books as $240.
- A $486 deposit by Acme Company was erroneously credited to our account by the bank.

McGraw-Hill/Irwin © 2004 The McGraw-Hill Companies

Bank Reconciliation

Ending bank balance, July 31		$ 9,610
Additions:		
Deposit in transit		500
Deductions:		
Bank error	$ 486	
Outstanding checks	2,417	2,903
Correct cash balance		$ 7,207

McGraw-Hill/Irwin © 2004 The McGraw-Hill Companies

Bank Reconciliation

Ending bank balance, July 31		$ 9,610
Additions:		
Deposit in transit		500
Deductions:		
Bank error	$ 486	
Outstanding checks	2,417	2,903
Correct cash balance		$ 7,207
Ending book balance, July 31		$ 7,430
Additions:		
Interest		30
Deductions:		
Recording error	$ 28	
NSF check	225	253
Correct cash balance		$ 7,207

McGraw-Hill/Irwin © 2004 The McGraw-Hill Companies

Bank Reconciliation

Date	Description	Post. Ref.	Debit	Credit
Jul 31	Cash		30	
	Interest Revenue			30
31	Supplies Inventory		28	
	Accounts Receivable		225	
	Cash			253

GENERAL JOURNAL — Page 56

McGraw-Hill/Irwin © 2004 The McGraw-Hill Companies

End of Chapter 6

McGraw-Hill/Irwin © 2004 The McGraw-Hill Companies

Chapter 7

Reporting and Interpreting
Cost of Goods Sold
and Inventory

Business Background

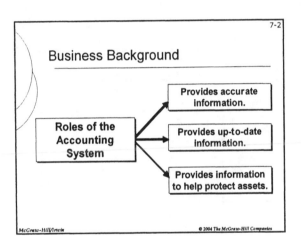

McGraw-Hill/Irwin   © 2004 The McGraw-Hill Companies

Nature of Inventory and Cost of Goods Sold

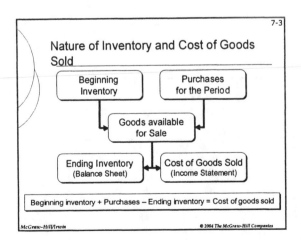

McGraw-Hill/Irwin   © 2004 The McGraw-Hill Companies

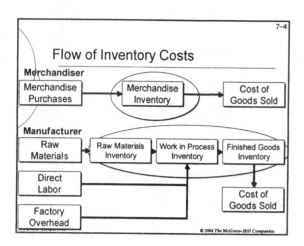

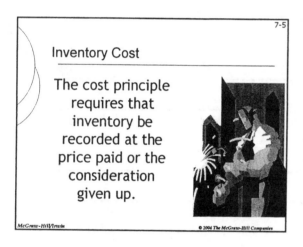

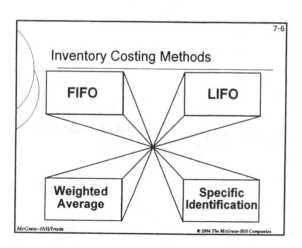

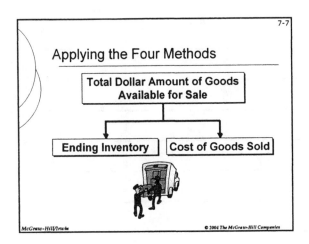

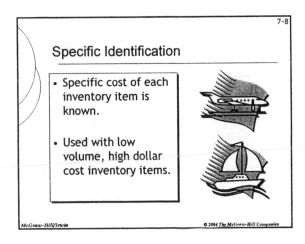

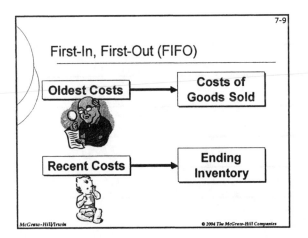

First-In, First-Out

The schedule on the next screen shows the mouse pad inventory for Computers, Inc.

The physical inventory count shows 1,200 mouse pads in ending inventory.

Use the FIFO inventory method to determine:

      (1) Ending inventory cost.

      (2) Cost of goods sold.

McGraw-Hill/Irwin   © 2004 The McGraw-Hill Companies

Computers, Inc.
Mouse Pad Inventory

Date	Units	$/Unit	Total
Beginning Inventory	1,000	$ 5.25	$ 5,250.00
Purchases:			
Jan. 3	300	5.30	1,590.00
June 20	150	5.60	840.00
Sept. 15	200	5.80	1,160.00
Nov. 29	150	5.90	885.00
Goods Available for Sale	1,800		$ 9,725.00
Ending Inventory	1200		?
Cost of Goods Sold	600		?

Remember: The costs of most recent purchases are in ending inventory. Start with 11/29 and add units purchased until you reach the number in ending inventory.

McGraw-Hill/Irwin   © 2004 The McGraw-Hill Companies

First-In, First-Out

Date	Beg. Inv.	Purchases	End. Inv.	Cost of Goods Sold
Nov. 29 Units		150@$5.90	150@$5.90 150	

McGraw-Hill/Irwin   © 2004 The McGraw-Hill Companies

First-In, First-Out

Date	Beg. Inv.	Purchases	End. Inv.	Cost of Goods Sold
Sept. 15		200@$5.80	200@$5.80	
Nov. 29		150@$5.90	150@$5.90	
Units			350	

McGraw-Hill/Irwin   © 2004 The McGraw-Hill Companies

First-In, First-Out

Date	Beg. Inv.	Purchases	End. Inv.	Cost of Goods Sold
June 20		150@$5.60	150@$5.60	
Sept. 15		200@$5.80	200@$5.80	
Nov. 29		150@$5.90	150@$5.90	
Units			500	

McGraw-Hill/Irwin   © 2004 The McGraw-Hill Companies

First-In, First-Out

Date	Beg. Inv.	Purchases	End. Inv.	Cost of Goods Sold
Jan. 3		300@$5.30	300@$5.30	
June 20		150@$5.60	150@$5.60	
Sept. 15		200@$5.80	200@$5.80	
Nov. 29		150@$5.90	150@$5.90	
Units			800	

McGraw-Hill/Irwin   © 2004 The McGraw-Hill Companies

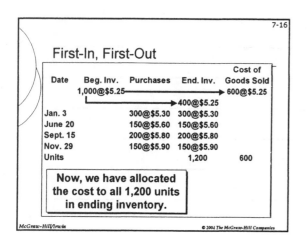

First-In, First-Out

Date	Beg. Inv.	Purchases	End. Inv.	Cost of Goods Sold
	1,000@$5.25			600@$5.25
			400@$5.25	
Jan. 3		300@$5.30	300@$5.30	
June 20		150@$5.60	150@$5.60	
Sept. 15		200@$5.80	200@$5.80	
Nov. 29		150@$5.90	150@$5.90	
Units			1,200	600

Now, we have allocated the cost to all 1,200 units in ending inventory.

McGraw-Hill/Irwin © 2004 The McGraw-Hill Companies

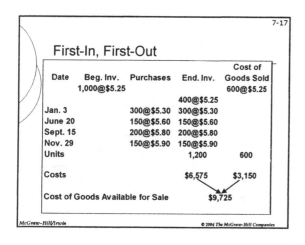

First-In, First-Out

Date	Beg. Inv.	Purchases	End. Inv.	Cost of Goods Sold
	1,000@$5.25			600@$5.25
			400@$5.25	
Jan. 3		300@$5.30	300@$5.30	
June 20		150@$5.60	150@$5.60	
Sept. 15		200@$5.80	200@$5.80	
Nov. 29		150@$5.90	150@$5.90	
Units			1,200	600
Costs			$6,575	$3,150
Cost of Goods Available for Sale			$9,725	

McGraw-Hill/Irwin © 2004 The McGraw-Hill Companies

ANY QUESTIONS BEFORE WE DISCUSS LIFO?

McGraw-Hill/Irwin © 2004 The McGraw-Hill Companies

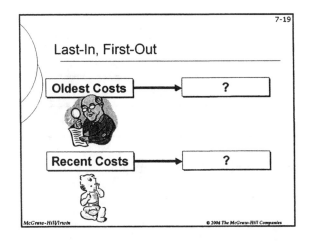

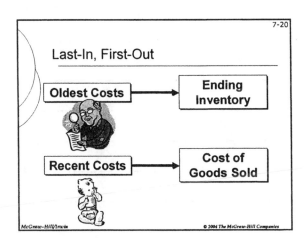

7-21

Last-In, First-Out

The schedule on the next screen shows the mouse pad inventory for Computers, Inc.

The physical inventory count shows 1,200 mouse pads in ending inventory.

Use the LIFO inventory method to determine:

    (1) Ending inventory cost.

    (2) Cost of goods sold.

McGraw-Hill/Irwin © 2004 The McGraw-Hill Companies

Computers, Inc. Mouse Pad Inventory			
Date	Units	$/Unit	Total
Beginning Inventory	1,000	$ 5.25	$ 5,250.00
Purchases:			
Jan. 3	300	5.30	1,590.00
June 20	150	5.60	840.00
Sept. 15	200	5.80	1,160.00
Nov. 29	150	5.90	885.00
Goods Available for Sale	1,800		$ 9,725.00
Ending Inventory	1200		?
Cost of Goods Sold	600		?

Remember: The costs of the oldest purchases are in ending inventory. Start with beginning inventory and add units purchased until you reach the number in ending inventory.

© 2004 The McGraw-Hill Companies

7-23

Last-In, First-Out

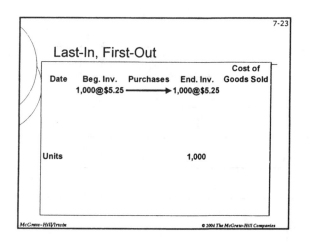

Date	Beg. Inv.	Purchases	End. Inv.	Cost of Goods Sold
	1,000@$5.25	⟶	1,000@$5.25	
Units			1,000	

McGraw-Hill/Irwin © 2004 The McGraw-Hill Companies

7-24

Last-In, First-Out

Date	Beg. Inv.	Purchases	End. Inv.	Cost of Goods Sold
	1,000@$5.25		1,000@$5.25	
Jan. 3		300@$5.30	200@$5.30	
Units			1,200	

Now, we have allocated the cost to all 1,200 units in ending inventory.

McGraw-Hill/Irwin © 2004 The McGraw-Hill Companies

Last-In, First-Out

Date	Beg. Inv.	Purchases	End. Inv.	Cost of Goods Sold
	1,000@$5.25		1,000@$5.25	
Jan. 3		300@$5.30	200@$5.30	
				100@$5.30
Units			1,200	100

Last-In, First-Out

Date	Beg. Inv.	Purchases	End. Inv.	Cost of Goods Sold
	1,000@$5.25		1,000@$5.25	
Jan. 3		300@$5.30	200@$5.30	
				100@$5.30
June 20		150@$5.60		150@$5.60
Sept. 15		200@$5.80		200@$5.80
Nov. 29		150@$5.90		150@$5.90
Units			1,200	600
Costs			$6,310	$3,415
Cost of Goods Available for Sale			$9,725	

Average Cost Method

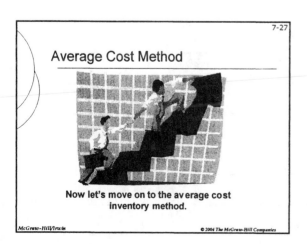

Now let's move on to the average cost inventory method.

Average Cost Method

7-28

Average cost per unit

$$\frac{\text{Cost of goods available for sale}}{\text{Number of units available for sale}}$$

Ending Inventory

Units in Ending Inventory × Average cost per Unit

Cost of Good Sold

Units Sold × Average cost per Unit

McGraw-Hill/Irwin   © 2004 The McGraw-Hill Companies

Average Cost Method

7-29

The schedule on the next screen shows the mouse pad inventory for Computers, Inc.

The physical inventory count shows 1,200 mouse pads in ending inventory.

Use the average cost inventory method to determine:

(1) Ending inventory cost.

(2) Cost of goods sold.

McGraw-Hill/Irwin   © 2004 The McGraw-Hill Companies

7-30

Computers, Inc. Mouse Pad Inventory			
Date	Units	$/Unit	Total
Beginning Inventory	1,000	$ 5.25	$ 5,250.00
Purchases:			
Jan. 3	300	5.30	1,590.00
June 20	150	5.60	840.00
Sept. 15	200	5.80	1,160.00
Nov. 29	150	5.90	885.00
Goods Available for Sale	1,800		$ 9,725.00
Ending Inventory	1200		?
Cost of Goods Sold	600		?

McGraw-Hill/Irwin   © 2004 The McGraw-Hill Companies

Weighted-Average

Weighted-Average Cost per Unit:

$$\frac{\$9,725}{1,800} = \$5.40278$$

Ending Inventory:

1,200 Units × $5.40278 = $6,483*

Cost of Goods Sold:

600 Units × $5.40278 = $3,242*

* Rounded

McGraw-Hill/Irwin © 2004 The McGraw-Hill Companies

Comparison of Methods

Computers, Inc.
Income Statement
For Year Ended December 31, 2003

	Average	FIFO	LIFO
Net sales	$ 25,000	$ 25,000	$ 25,000
Cost of goods sold:			
Merchandise inventory, 12/31/02	$ 5,250	$ 5,250	$ 5,250
Net purchases	4,475	4,475	4,475
Goods available for sale	$ 9,725	$ 9,725	$ 9,725
Merchandise inventory, 12/31/03	6,483	6,575	6,310
Cost of goods sold	$ 3,242	$ 3,150	$ 3,415
Gross profit from sales	$ 21,758	$ 21,850	$ 21,585
Operating expenses:	750	750	750
Income before taxes	$ 21,008	$ 21,100	$ 20,835
Income taxes expense (30%)*	6,302	6,330	6,251
Net income	$ 14,706	$ 14,770	$ 14,584

McGraw- * Tax expense amounts were rounded.

In periods of rising prices, FIFO results in the highest ending inventory, gross profit, tax expense, and net income, and the lowest cost of goods sold.

31, 2003

	Average	FIFO	LIFO
Net sales	$ 25,000	$ 25,000	$ 25,000
Cost of goods sold:			
Merchandise inventory, 12/31/02	$ 5,250	$ 5,250	$ 5,250
Net purchases	4,475	4,475	4,475
Goods available for sale	$ 9,725	$ 9,725	$ 9,725
Merchandise inventory, 12/31/03	6,483	6,575	6,310
Cost of goods sold	$ 3,242	$ 3,150	$ 3,415
Gross profit from sales	$ 21,758	$ 21,850	$ 21,585
Operating expenses:	750	750	750
Income before taxes	$ 21,008	$ 21,100	$ 20,835
Income taxes expense (30%)*	6,302	6,330	6,251
Net income	$ 14,706	$ 14,770	$ 14,584

McGraw- * Tax expense amounts were rounded.

In periods of rising prices, LIFO results in the lowest ending inventory, gross profit, tax expense, and net income, and the highest cost of goods sold.

	Average	FIFO	LIFO
Net sales	$ 25,000	$ 25,000	$ 25,000
Cost of goods sold:			
Merchandise inventory, 12/31/02	$ 5,250	$ 5,250	$ 5,250
Net purchases	4,475	4,475	4,475
Goods available for sale	$ 9,725	$ 9,725	$ 9,725
Merchandise inventory, 12/31/03	6,483	6,575	6,310
Cost of goods sold	$ 3,242	$ 3,150	$ 3,415
Gross profit from sales	$ 21,758	$ 21,850	$ 21,585
Operating expenses:	750	750	750
Income before taxes	$ 21,008	$ 21,100	$ 20,835
Income taxes expense (30%)*	6,302	6,330	6,251
Net income	$ 14,706	$ 14,770	$ 14,584

McGraw- * Tax expense amounts were rounded.

Choosing Inventory Costing Methods

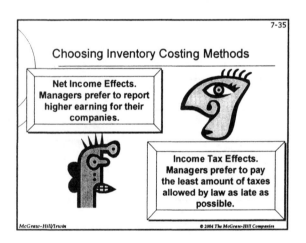

Net Income Effects. Managers prefer to report higher earning for their companies.

Income Tax Effects. Managers prefer to pay the least amount of taxes allowed by law as late as possible.

McGraw-Hill/Irwin   © 2004 The McGraw-Hill Companies

Choosing Inventory Costing Methods

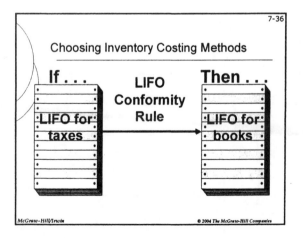

If . . .   LIFO   **Then . . .**
            Conformity
·LIFO for·   Rule   ·LIFO for·
· taxes ·   · books ·

McGraw-Hill/Irwin   © 2004 The McGraw-Hill Companies

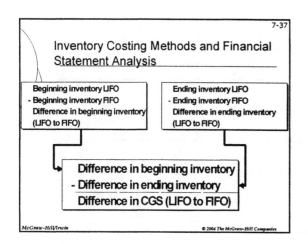

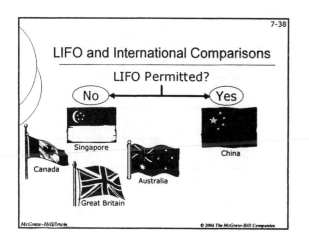

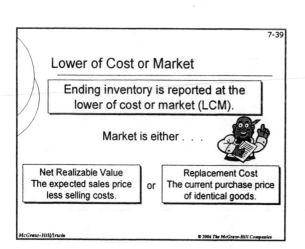

Lower of Cost or Market

Mouse pads	Cost	Total Cost	Replacement Cost	Total Market	LCM
1,600	$ 5.20	$ 8,320	$ 4.15	$ 6,640	$ 6,640

The mouse pads will be shown on the balance sheet at $6,640 (LCM). The company will recognize a "holding" loss in the current period rather than the period in which the item is sold.
This practice is conservative.

Measuring Efficiency in Inventory Management

Inventory Turnover

$$\text{Inventory Turnover} = \frac{\text{Cost of Goods Sold}}{\text{Average Inventory}}$$

Average Inventory is . . .
(Beginning Inventory + Ending Inventory) ÷ 2

This ratio is often used to measure the liquidity (nearness to cash) of the inventory.

Measuring Efficiency in Inventory Management

Inventory Turnover

$$\text{Inventory Turnover} = \frac{\text{Cost of Goods Sold}}{\text{Average Inventory}}$$

The 2000 inventory turnover ratio for Harley-Davidson:

$$\frac{\$1,915,547}{(\$191,931 + \$168,616) \div 2} = 10.6$$

7-43

Focus on Cash Flows

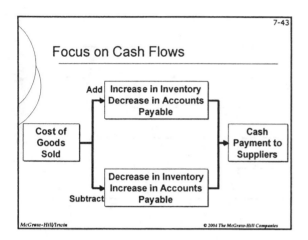

7-44

Errors in Measuring Inventory

Errors in Measuring Inventory

	Beginning Inventory		Ending Inventory	
	Overstated	Understated	Overstated	Understated
Effect on Income Statement				
Goods Available for Sale	+	-	N/A	N/A
Cost of Goods Sold	+	-	-	+
Gross Profit	-	+	+	-
Net Income	-	+	+	-
Effect on Balance Sheet				
Inventory (12/31)	N/A	N/A	+	-
Retained Earnings	-	+	+	-

7-45

Question

If the 2002 ending inventory is understated by $3,000, which of the following is true for 2002?

a. Beginning Inventory was understated.
b. Cost of Goods Sold will be understated.
c. Gross Profit will be overstated.
d. Net Income will be understated.

Slide 7-46

Question

If the 2002 ending inventory is understated by $3,000, which of the following is true for 2~~

Errors in Measuring Inventory		
	Ending Inventory	
	Overstated	Understated
Effect on Income Statement		
Goods Available for Sale	N/A	N/A
Cost of Goods Sold	-	+
Gross Profit	+	-
Net Income	+	-
Effect on Balance Sheet		
Inventory (12/31)	+	-
Retained Earnings	+	-

a. Beginning Inventory
b. Cost of Goods Sold w~~
c. Gross Profit will be ~~
d. Net Income will be understated.

Slide 7-47

Question

If the 2002 ending inventory is understated by $3,000, which of the following is true for 2003?

a. Beginning Inventory was understated.
b. Cost of Goods Sold will be understated.
c. Gross Profit will be overstated.
d. All of the above.

Slide 7-48

Question

If the 2002 ending inventory is understated by $3,000, which of the following is true for 2003?

a. Beginning Inventory was understated.
b. Cost of Goods Sold will be understated.
c. Gross Profit will be overstated.
d. All of the above.

Remember: The ending inventory for 2002 becomes the beginning inventory for 2003.

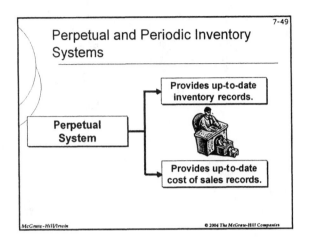

Perpetual and Periodic Inventory Systems

Perpetual System → Provides up-to-date inventory records.

Provides up-to-date cost of sales records.

McGraw-Hill/Irwin © 2004 The McGraw-Hill Companies

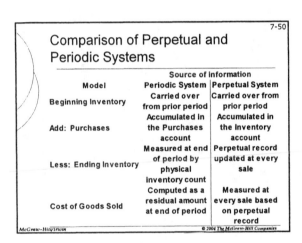

7-50

Comparison of Perpetual and Periodic Systems

Model	Source of Information	
	Periodic System	Perpetual System
Beginning Inventory	Carried over from prior period	Carried over from prior period
Add: Purchases	Accumulated in the Purchases account	Accumulated in the Inventory account
Less: Ending Inventory	Measured at end of period by physical inventory count	Perpetual record updated at every sale
Cost of Goods Sold	Computed as a residual amount at end of period	Measured at every sale based on perpetual record

McGraw-Hill/Irwin © 2004 The McGraw-Hill Companies

7-51

The End of Chapter 7

McGraw-Hill/Irwin © 2004 The McGraw-Hill Companies

Chapter 8

Reporting and Interpreting Property, Plant, and Equipment; Natural Resources; and Intangibles

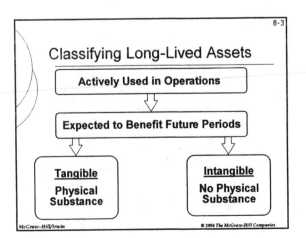

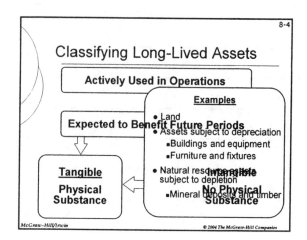

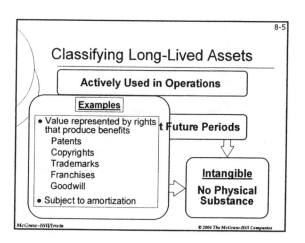

Fixed Asset Turnover

$$\text{Fixed Asset Turnover} = \frac{\text{Net Sales Revenue}}{\text{Average Net Fixed Assets}}$$

For the year 2000, Delta Airlines had $16,741 of revenue. End-of-year fixed assets were $14,840 and beginning-of-year fixed assets were $12,450. (All numbers in millions.)

This ratio measures a company's ability to generate sales given an investment in fixed assets.

McGraw-Hill/Irwin   © 2004 The McGraw-Hill Companies

8-7

Fixed Asset Turnover

$$\frac{\text{Fixed}}{\text{Asset}} = \frac{\text{Net Sales Revenue}}{\text{Average Net Fixed Assets}}$$

$$\frac{\text{Fixed}}{\text{Asset}} = \frac{\$16,741}{(\$14,840 + \$12,450) \div 2} = 1.23$$

2000 Fixed Asset Turnover Comparisons		
Delta	Southwest	United
1.23	1.04	1.47

McGraw-Hill/Irwin © 2004 The McGraw-Hill Companies

8-8

Measuring and Recording Acquisition Cost

Acquisition cost includes the purchase price and all expenditures needed to prepare the asset for its intended use.

Acquisition cost does not include financing charges and cash discounts.

McGraw-Hill/Irwin © 2004 The McGraw-Hill Companies

8-9

Acquisition Cost
Buildings

- Purchase price
- Architectural fees
- Cost of permits
- Excavation costs
- Construction costs

McGraw-Hill/Irwin © 2004 The McGraw-Hill Companies

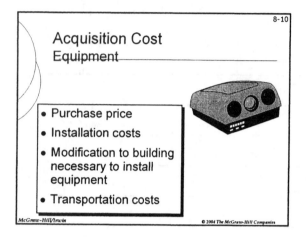

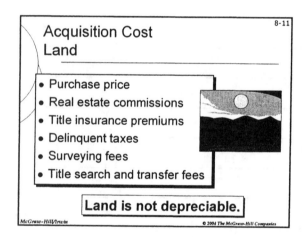

Acquisition for Cash

On June 1, Delta Air Lines purchased aircraft for $60,000,000 cash.

GENERAL JOURNAL			Page 8
Date	Description	Debit	Credit
June 1			

McGraw-Hill/Irwin   © 2004 The McGraw-Hill Companies

8-5

Acquisition for Cash

8-13

On June 1, Delta Air Lines purchased aircraft for $60,000,000 cash.

GENERAL JOURNAL			Page 8	
Date		Description	Debit	Credit
June	1	Flight equipment	60,000,000	
		Cash		60,000,000

Acquisition for Debt

8-14

On June 14, Delta Air Lines purchased aircraft for $1,000,000 cash and a $59,000,000 note payable.

GENERAL JOURNAL			Page 9	
Date		Description	Debit	Credit
June	14			

Acquisition for Debt

8-15

On June 14, Delta Air Lines purchased aircraft for $1,000,000 cash and a $59,000,000 note payable.

GENERAL JOURNAL			Page 9	
Date		Description	Debit	Credit
June	14	Flight equipment	60,000,000	
		Cash		1,000,000
		Note payable		59,000,000

Acquisition for Noncash Consideration

Record at the current market value of the consideration given, or the current market value of the asset acquired, whichever is more clearly evident.

McGraw-Hill/Irwin

© 2004 The McGraw-Hill Companies

Acquisition for Noncash Consideration

On July 7, Delta gave Boeing 400,000 shares of $3 par value common stock with a market value of $85 per share plus $26,000,000 in cash for aircraft.

GENERAL JOURNAL				Page 10
Date		Description	Debit	Credit
July	7			

McGraw-Hill/Irwin

© 2004 The McGraw-Hill Companies

Acquisition for Noncash Consideration

On July 7, Delta gave Boeing 400,000 shares of $3 par value common stock with a market value of $85 per share plus $26,000,000 in cash for aircraft.

GENERAL JOURNAL				Page 10
Date		Description	Debit	Credit
July	7	Flight equipment	60,000,000	
		Cash		26,000,000
		Common stock		1,200,000
		Additional paid-in capital		32,800,000

McGraw-Hill/Irwin

© 2004 The McGraw-Hill Companies

Acquisition by Construction

8-19

Asset cost includes:

| All materials and labor traceable to the construction. | A reasonable amount of overhead. | Interest on debt incurred during the construction. |

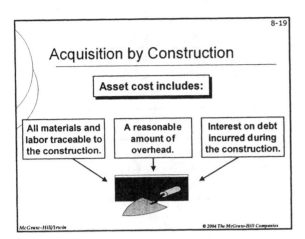

Repairs, Maintenance, and Additions

8-20

Type of Expenditure	Capital or Revenue	Identifying Characteristics
Ordinary repairs and maintenance	Revenue	1. Maintains normal operating condition 2. Does not increase productivity 3. Does not extend life beyond original estimate
Extraordinary repairs	Capital	1. Major overhauls or partial replacements 2. Extends life beyond original estimate
Additions	Capital	1. Increases productivity 2. May extend useful life 3. Improvements or expansions

---

Capital and Revenue Expenditures

8-21

	Financial Statement Effect			
Treatment	Statement	Expense	Current Income	Current Taxes
Capital Expenditure	Balance sheet account debited	Deferred	Higher	Higher
Revenue Expenditure	Income statement account debited	Currently recognized	Lower	Lower

Many companies have policies expensing all expenditures below a certain amount according to the materiality constraint.

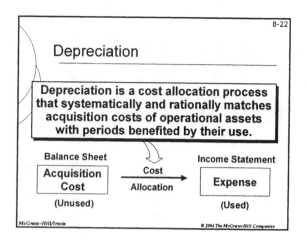

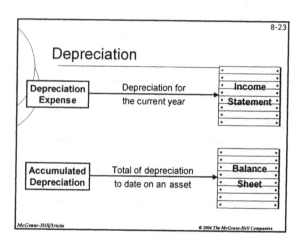

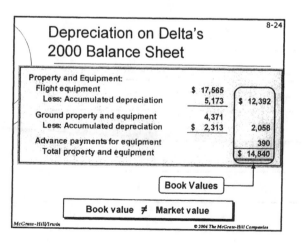

8-9

8-25

Depreciation Concepts

The calculation of depreciation requires three amounts for each asset:

❶ **Acquisition cost.**

❷ **Estimated useful life.**

❸ **Estimated residual value.**

McGraw-Hill/Irwin   © 2004 The McGraw-Hill Companies

8-26

Alternative Depreciation Methods

❶ Straight-line

❷ Units-of-production

❸ Accelerated Method: Declining balance

McGraw-Hill/Irwin   © 2004 The McGraw-Hill Companies

8-27

Straight-Line Method

| Depreciation Expense per Year | = | Cost - Residual Value / Life in Years |

At the beginning of the year, Delta purchased equipment for $62,500 cash. The equipment has an estimated useful life of 3 years and an estimated residual value of $2,500.

SL

McGraw-Hill/Irwin   © 2004 The McGraw-Hill Companies

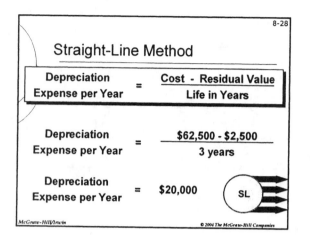

Straight-Line Method

$$\frac{\text{Depreciation}}{\text{Expense per Year}} = \frac{\text{Cost - Residual Value}}{\text{Life in Years}}$$

$$\frac{\text{Depreciation}}{\text{Expense per Year}} = \frac{\$62,500 - \$2,500}{3 \text{ years}}$$

$$\frac{\text{Depreciation}}{\text{Expense per Year}} = \$20,000 \quad \text{SL}$$

McGraw-Hill/Irwin   © 2004 The McGraw-Hill Companies

Straight-Line Method

Year	Depreciation Expense (debit)	Accumulated Depreciation (credit)	Accumulated Depreciation Balance	Undepreciated Balance (book value)
				$ 62,500
1	$ 20,000	$ 20,000	$ 20,000	42,500
2	20,000	20,000	40,000	22,500
3	20,000	20,000	60,000	2,500
	$ 60,000	$ 60,000		

Residual Value

SL

More than 95 percent of companies use the straight-line method for some or all of their assets disclosed in financial reports.

McGraw-Hill/Irwin   © 2004 The McGraw-Hill Companies

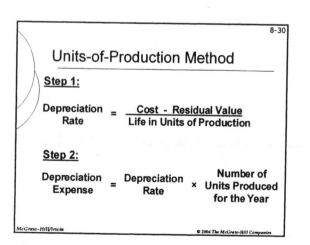

Units-of-Production Method

Step 1:

$$\frac{\text{Depreciation}}{\text{Rate}} = \frac{\text{Cost - Residual Value}}{\text{Life in Units of Production}}$$

Step 2:

$$\frac{\text{Depreciation}}{\text{Expense}} = \frac{\text{Depreciation}}{\text{Rate}} \times \frac{\text{Number of}}{\text{Units Produced for the Year}}$$

McGraw-Hill/Irwin   © 2004 The McGraw-Hill Companies

Units-of-Production Method

At the beginning of the year, Delta purchased ground equipment for $62,500 cash. The equipment has a 100,000 mile useful life and an estimated residual value of $2,500.

If the equipment is used 30,000 miles in the first year, what is the amount of depreciation expense?

McGraw-Hill/Irwin   © 2004 The McGraw-Hill Companies

Units-of-Production Method

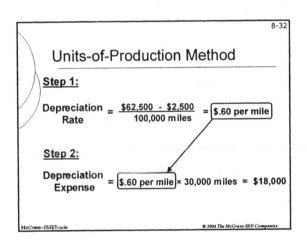

Step 1:

$$\text{Depreciation Rate} = \frac{\$62,500 - \$2,500}{100,000 \text{ miles}} = \boxed{\$.60 \text{ per mile}}$$

Step 2:

$$\text{Depreciation Expense} = \boxed{\$.60 \text{ per mile}} \times 30,000 \text{ miles} = \$18,000$$

McGraw-Hill/Irwin   © 2004 The McGraw-Hill Companies

Units-of-Production Method

Year	Miles	Depreciation Expense	Accumulated Depreciation Balance	Undepreciated Balance (book value)
				$ 62,500
1	30,000	$ 18,000	$ 18,000	44,500
2	50,000			
3	20,000			
	100,000			

McGraw-Hill/Irwin   © 2004 The McGraw-Hill Companies

Units-of-Production Method

Year	Miles	Depreciation Expense	Accumulated Depreciation Balance	Undepreciated Balance (book value)
				$ 62,500
1	30,000	$ 18,000	$ 18,000	44,500
2	50,000	30,000	48,000	14,500
3	20,000	12,000	60,000	2,500
	100,000	$ 60,000		

Residual Value

© 2004 The McGraw-Hill Companies

Accelerated Depreciation

Accelerated depreciation matches higher depreciation expense with higher revenues in the early years of an asset's useful life when the asset is more efficient.

	Depreciation Expense	Repair Expense
Early Years	High	Low
Later Years	Low	High

© 2004 The McGraw-Hill Companies

Double-Declining-Balance Method

Declining balance rate of 2 is double-declining-balance (DDB) rate.

$$\text{Annual Depreciation expense} = \text{Net Book Value} \times \left(\frac{2}{\text{Useful Life in Years}} \right)$$

Cost – Accumulated Depreciation

Annual computation ignores residual value.

© 2004 The McGraw-Hill Companies

Double-Declining-Balance Method

At the beginning of the year, Delta purchased equipment for $62,500 cash. The equipment has an estimated useful life of 3 years and an estimated residual value of $2,500.

Calculate the depreciation expense for the first two years.

McGraw-Hill/Irwin   © 2004 The McGraw-Hill Companies

Double-Declining-Balance Method

$$\text{Annual Depreciation expense} = \text{Net Book Value} \times \left(\frac{2}{\text{Useful Life in Years}} \right)$$

Year 1 Depreciation:

$$\$62,500 \times \left(\frac{2}{3 \text{ years}} \right) = \boxed{\$41,667}$$

Year 2 Depreciation:

$$(\$62,500 - \boxed{\$41,667}) \times \left(\frac{2}{3 \text{ years}} \right) = \$13,889$$

McGraw-Hill/Irwin   © 2004 The McGraw-Hill Companies

Double-Declining-Balance Method

Year	Depreciation Expense (debit)	Accumulated Depreciation Balance	Undepreciated Balance (book value)
			$ 62,500
1	$ 41,667	$ 41,667	20,833
2	13,889	55,556	6,944
3	4,629	60,185	2,315
	$ 60,185		

Below residual value

$$(\$62,500 - \$55,556) \times \left(\frac{2}{3 \text{ years}} \right) = \$4,629$$

McGraw-Hill/Irwin   © 2004 The McGraw-Hill Companies

Double-Declining-Balance Method

8-40

Year	Depreciation Expense (debit)	Accumulated Depreciation Balance	Undepreciated Balance (book value)
			$ 62,500
1	$ 41,667	$ 41,667	20,833
2	13,889	55,556	6,944
3	4,444	60,000	2,500
	$ 60,000		

Depreciation expense is limited to the amount that reduces book value to the estimated residual value.

McGraw-Hill/Irwin   © 2004 The McGraw-Hill Companies

Depreciation and Federal Income Tax

8-41

For tax purposes, most corporations use the Modified Accelerated Cost Recovery System (MACRS).

MACRS depreciation provides for rapid write-off of an asset's cost in order to stimulate new investment.

McGraw-Hill/Irwin   © 2004 The McGraw-Hill Companies

Depreciation Methods in Other Countries

8-42

Many countries, including Australia, Brazil, England, and Mexico, use other methods such as depreciation based on the current fair value of assets.

McGraw-Hill/Irwin   © 2004 The McGraw-Hill Companies

Asset Impairment

8-43

Impairment is the loss of a significant portion of the utility of an asset through . . .

- Casualty.
- Obsolescence.
- Lack of demand for the asset's services.

A loss should be recognized when an asset suffers a permanent impairment.

McGraw-Hill/Irwin   © 2004 The McGraw-Hill Companies

Disposal of Property, Plant, and Equipment

8-44

Voluntary disposals:
- Sale
- Trade-in
- Retirement

Involuntary disposals:
- Fire
- Accident

McGraw-Hill/Irwin   © 2004 The McGraw-Hill Companies

Disposal of Property, Plant, and Equipment

8-45

❶ Update depreciation to the date of disposal.

❷ Journalize disposal by:

Recording cash received (debit) or paid (credit).	Recording a gain (credit) or loss (debit).
Writing off accumulated depreciation (debit).	Writing off the asset cost (credit).

McGraw-Hill/Irwin   © 2004 The McGraw-Hill Companies

Disposal of Property, Plant, and Equipment

8-46

If Cash > BV, record a gain (credit).

If Cash < BV, record a loss (debit).

If Cash = BV, no gain or loss.

McGraw-Hill/Irwin

© 2004 The McGraw-Hill Companies

Disposal of Property, Plant, and Equipment

8-47

Delta Airlines sold flight equipment for $5,000,000 cash at the end of its 17th year of use. The flight equipment originally cost $20,000,000, and was depreciated using the straight-line method with zero salvage value and a useful life of 20 years.

McGraw-Hill/Irwin

© 2004 The McGraw-Hill Companies

Disposal of Property, Plant, and Equipment

8-48

The amount of depreciation recorded at the end of the 17th year to bring depreciation up to date is:

a. $0.

b. $1,000,000.

c. $2,000,000.

d. $4,000,000.

McGraw-Hill/Irwin

© 2004 The McGraw-Hill Companies

Disposal of Property, Plant, and Equipment

The amount of depreciation recorded at the end of the 17th year to bring depreciation up to date is:

a. $0.

b. $1,000,000.

c. $2,000,000.

d. $4,000,000.

Annual Depreciation:
($20,000,000 - $0) ÷ 20 Years.
= $1,000,000

McGraw-Hill/Irwin © 2004 The McGraw-Hill Companies

Disposal of Property, Plant, and Equipment

After updating the depreciation, the equipment's book value at the end of the 17th year is:

a. $3,000,000.

b. $16,000,000.

c. $17,000,000.

d. $4,000,000.

McGraw-Hill/Irwin © 2004 The McGraw-Hill Companies

Disposal of Property, Plant, and Equipment

After up **the equip** **end**

Accumulated Depreciation =
(17yrs. × $1,000,000) = $17,000,000
BV = Cost - Accumulated Depreciation
BV = $20,000,000 - $17,000,000
= $3,000,000

a. $3,000,000.

b. $16,000,000.

c. $17,000,000.

d. $4,000,000.

McGraw-Hill/Irwin © 2004 The McGraw-Hill Companies

Disposal of Property, Plant, and Equipment

8-52

The equipment's sale resulted in:

a. a gain of $2,000,000.
b. a gain of $3,000,000.
c. a gain of $4,000,000.
d. a loss of $2,000,000.

McGraw-Hill/Irwin © 2004 The McGraw-Hill Companies

Disposal of Property, Plant, and Equipment

8-53

The equipment's sale resulted in:

a. a gain of $2,000,000.
b. a gain of $3,000,000.
c. a gain of $4,000,000.
d. a loss of $2,000,000.

Gain = Cash Received - Book Value
Gain = $5,000,000 - $3,000,000 = $2,000,000

McGraw-Hill/Irwin © 2004 The McGraw-Hill Companies

Disposal of Property, Plant, and Equipment

8-54

Prepare the journal entry to record Delta's sale of the equipment at the end of the 17th year.

GENERAL JOURNAL		Page 8	
Date	Description	Debit	Credit

McGraw-Hill/Irwin © 2004 The McGraw-Hill Companies

Disposal of Property, Plant, and Equipment

Prepare the journal entry to record Delta's sale of the equipment at the end of the 17th year.

	GENERAL JOURNAL			Page 8
Date	Description		Debit	Credit
	Cash		5,000,000	
	Accumulated Depreciation		17,000,000	
		Gain on Sale		2,000,000
		Flight Equipment		20,000,000

McGraw-Hill/Irwin © 2004 The McGraw-Hill Companies

Natural Resources

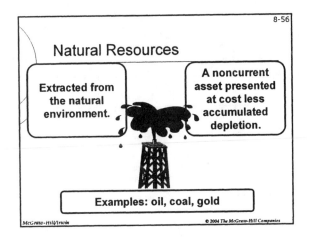

Extracted from the natural environment.

A noncurrent asset presented at cost less accumulated depletion.

Examples: oil, coal, gold

McGraw-Hill/Irwin © 2004 The McGraw-Hill Companies

Natural Resources

Total cost of asset is the cost of acquisition, exploration, and development.

Total cost is allocated over periods benefited by means of depletion.

Depletion is like depreciation.

McGraw-Hill/Irwin © 2004 The McGraw-Hill Companies

Depletion of Natural Resources

Depletion is calculated using the units-of-production method.

Unit depletion rate is calculated as follows:

$$\frac{\text{Acquisition and Development Cost} - \text{Residual Value}}{\text{Estimated Recoverable Units}}$$

Depletion of Natural Resources

Total depletion cost for a period is:

UNIT DEPLETION RATE **×** NUMBER OF UNITS EXTRACTED IN PERIOD

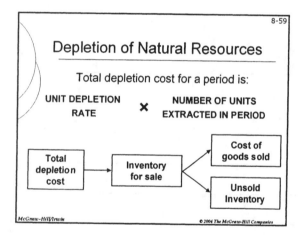

Natural Resources

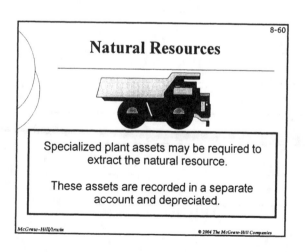

Specialized plant assets may be required to extract the natural resource.

These assets are recorded in a separate account and depreciated.

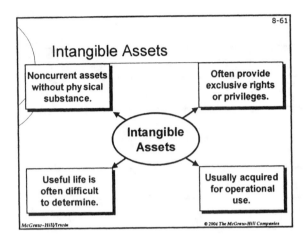

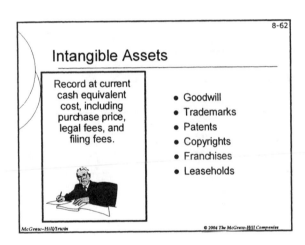

Intangible Assets

- **Amortize over shorter of economic life or legal life, subject to rules specified by GAAP.**
- **Use straight-line method.**
- **Research and development costs are normally expensed as incurred.**

McGraw-Hill/Irwin   © 2004 The McGraw-Hill Companies

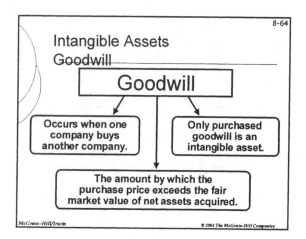

Intangible Assets
Goodwill

Goodwill

Occurs when one company buys another company.

Only purchased goodwill is an intangible asset.

The amount by which the purchase price exceeds the fair market value of net assets acquired.

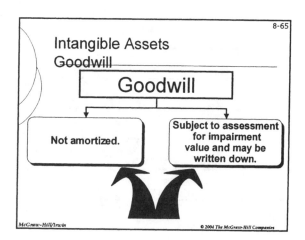

Intangible Assets
Goodwill

Goodwill

Not amortized.

Subject to assessment for impairment value and may be written down.

Intangible Assets
Goodwill

Eddy Company paid $1,000,000 to purchase all of James Company's assets and assumed liabilities of $200,000. The acquired assets were appraised at a fair value of $900,000.

8-67

Intangible Assets
Goodwill

What amount of goodwill should be recorded on Eddy Company books?

a. $100,000
b. $200,000
c. $300,000
d. $400,000

McGraw-Hill/Irwin © 2004 The McGraw-Hill Companies

8-68

Intangible Assets
Goodwill

What amount of goodwill should be recorded on Eddy Company books?

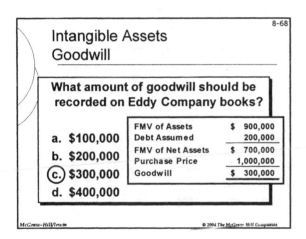

a. $100,000	FMV of Assets	$ 900,000
	Debt Assumed	200,000
b. $200,000	FMV of Net Assets	$ 700,000
	Purchase Price	1,000,000
(c.) $300,000	Goodwill	$ 300,000
d. $400,000		

McGraw-Hill/Irwin © 2004 The McGraw-Hill Companies

8-69

Intangible Assets
Trademarks

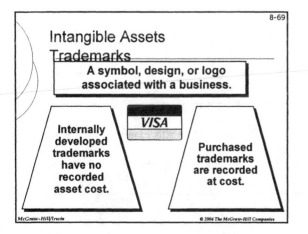

A symbol, design, or logo associated with a business.

VISA

Internally developed trademarks have no recorded asset cost.

Purchased trademarks are recorded at cost.

McGraw-Hill/Irwin © 2004 The McGraw-Hill Companies

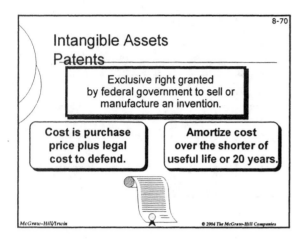

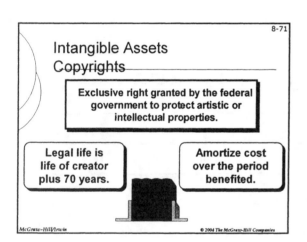

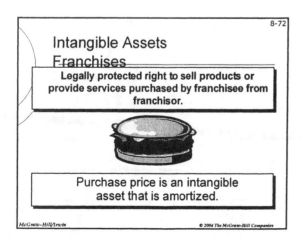

8-73

Intangible Assets
Leaseholds

- A lease is a contract to use property granted by lessor to lessee and rights granted under the lease are called a leasehold.

- A leasehold is recorded only if advance payment is involved. Otherwise periodic payments are rent expense.

© 2004 The McGraw-Hill Companies

8-74

Intangible Assets
Leasehold Improvements

> Long-lived alterations made by lessee to leased property.

Leasehold improvements are recorded at cost and amortized over their useful life.

© 2004 The McGraw-Hill Companies

8-75

This computer is about to become fully depreciated!

End of Chapter 8

© 2004 The McGraw-Hill Companies

Chapter 9

Reporting and Interpreting Liabilities

Understanding the Business

The acquisition of assets is financed from two sources:

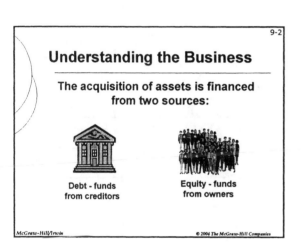

Debt - funds from creditors

Equity - funds from owners

Understanding the Business

Debt is considered riskier than equity.

Interest is a legal obligation.

Creditors can force bankruptcy.

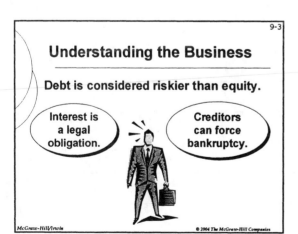

9-4

Liabilities Defined and Classified

Defined as probable debts or obligations of the entity that result from past transactions, which will be paid with assets or services.

Maturity = 1 year or less | Maturity > 1 year

Current Liabilities | Noncurrent Liabilities

McGraw-Hill/Irwin © 2004 The McGraw-Hill Companies

9-5

Liabilities Defined and Classified

Liabilities are measured at their current cash equivalent (the amount a creditor would accept to cancel the debt) at the time incurred.

McGraw-Hill/Irwin © 2004 The McGraw-Hill Companies

9-6

Liabilities Defined and Classified

An important indicator of a company's ability to meet its current obligations.

Two commonly used measures:

Current Ratio = Current Assets ÷ Current Liabilities

Working Capital = Current Assets - Current Liabilities

McGraw-Hill/Irwin © 2004 The McGraw-Hill Companies

Current Ratio

General Mills has current assets of $1,190.30 and current liabilities of $2,529.10.

The current ratio is . . .

Current Ratio	=	Current Assets	÷	Current Liabilities
	=	$1,190.30	÷	$2,529.10
	=	0.47		

McGraw-Hill/Irwin © 2004 The McGraw-Hill Companies

Current Liabilities

Account Name	Also Called	Definition
Accounts Payable	Trade Accounts Payable	Obligations to pay for goods and services used in the basic operating activities of the business.
Accrued Liabilities	Accrued Expenses	Obligations related to expenses that have been incurred, but will not be paid until the subsequent period.
Deferred Revenues	Unearned Revenues	Obligations arising when cash is received prior to the related revenue being earned.
Note Payable	N/A	Portions of debt that are due within the next year or operating cycle.

McGraw-Hill/Irwin © 2004 The McGraw-Hill Companies

Payroll Liabilities

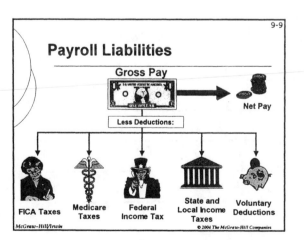

Gross Pay

Net Pay

Less Deductions:

FICA Taxes   Medicare Taxes   Federal Income Tax   State and Local Income Taxes   Voluntary Deductions

McGraw-Hill/Irwin © 2004 The McGraw-Hill Companies

Interest

Interest is the compensation to the lender for giving up the use of money for a period of time.
➢To the lender, interest is a revenue.
➢To the borrower, interest is an expense.

McGraw-Hill/Irwin   © 2004 The McGraw-Hill Companies

Interest

The interest formula includes three variables that must be considered when computing interest:

Interest = Principal × Interest Rate × Time

When computing interest for one year, "Time" equals 1. When the computation period is less than one year, then "Time" is a fraction.

McGraw-Hill/Irwin   © 2004 The McGraw-Hill Companies

Interest

General Mills borrows $100,000 for 2 months at an annual interest rate of 12%. Compute the interest on the note for the loan period.

McGraw-Hill/Irwin   © 2004 The McGraw-Hill Companies

Interest

General Mills borrows $100,000 for 2 months at an annual interest rate of 12%. Compute the interest on the note for the loan period.

Interest	=	Principal	×	Interest Rate	×	Time
Interest	=	$100,000	×	12%	×	2/12
Interest	=	$ 2,000				

Long-Term Liabilities

Creditors often require the borrower to pledge specific assets as security for the long-term liability.

Maturity = 1 year or less | Maturity > 1 year

Current Liabilities | Long-term Liabilities

Long-Term Debt

It's going to take my company years to pay for this project!

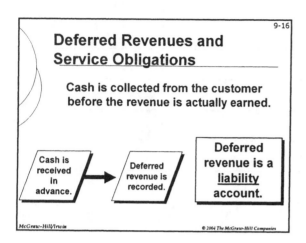

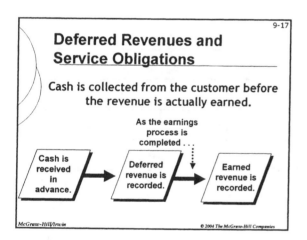

Contingent Liabilities

9-18

Potential liabilities that arise because of events or transactions that have already occurred.

Probability of future sacrifice . . .

	Probable	Reasonably Possible	Remote
Amount Can be Estimated	Record contingent liability.	Disclose liability in the notes to the financial stmts.	No action.
Amount Cannot be Estimated	Disclose liability in the notes to the financial stmts.	Disclose liability in the notes to the financial stmts.	No action.

McGraw-Hill/Irwin   © 2004 The McGraw-Hill Companies

Working Capital Management

Changes in working capital accounts affect cash flows as indicated in the following table.

| | Change in Account Balance During Year | |
	Increase	Decrease
Current Assets	Subtract from net income.	Add to net income.
Current Liabilities	Add to net income.	Subtract from net income.

McGraw-Hill/Irwin © 2004 The McGraw-Hill Companies

Sources for Long-Term Loans

Relatively small debt needs can be filled from single sources.

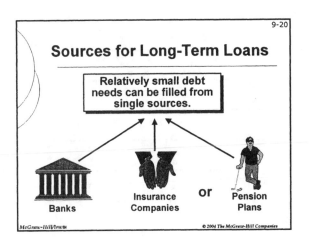

Banks   Insurance Companies   or   Pension Plans

McGraw-Hill/Irwin © 2004 The McGraw-Hill Companies

Sources for Publicly Issued Debt

Significant debt needs are often filled by issuing bonds to the public.

Bonds   Cash

McGraw-Hill/Irwin © 2004 The McGraw-Hill Companies

Borrowing in Foreign Currencies

- When a company has operations in a foreign country, it often borrows in the local currency. This reduces exchange rate risk.

- Because interest rates vary from country to country, companies may borrow in the foreign market with the lowest interest rate.

Now let's turn our attention to present value concepts.

Present and Future Value Concepts

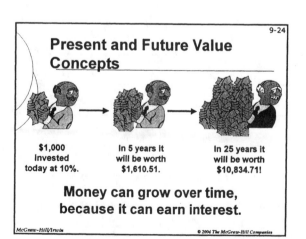

$1,000 invested today at 10%.

In 5 years it will be worth $1,610.51.

In 25 years it will be worth $10,834.71!

Money can grow over time, because it can earn interest.

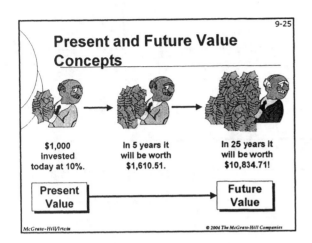

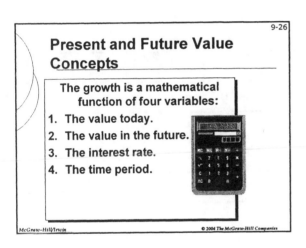

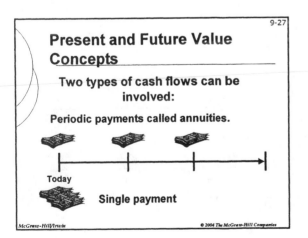

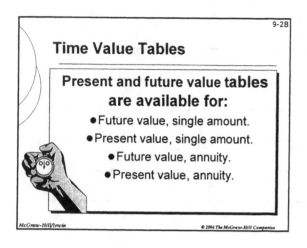

Time Value Tables

9-28

Present and future value tables are available for:
- Future value, single amount.
- Present value, single amount.
  - Future value, annuity.
  - Present value, annuity.

McGraw-Hill/Irwin   © 2004 The McGraw-Hill Companies

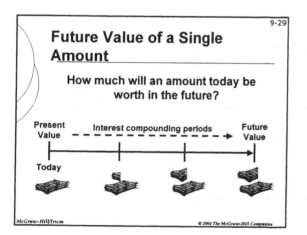

Future Value of a Single Amount

9-29

How much will an amount today be worth in the future?

Present Value ---- Interest compounding periods ----> Future Value

Today

McGraw-Hill/Irwin   © 2004 The McGraw-Hill Companies

Future Value of a Single Amount

9-30

If we invest $1,000 today earning 10% interest, compounded annually, how much will it be worth in three (3) years?

a. $1,000
b. $1,010
c. $1,100
d. $1,331

McGraw-Hill/Irwin   © 2004 The McGraw-Hill Companies

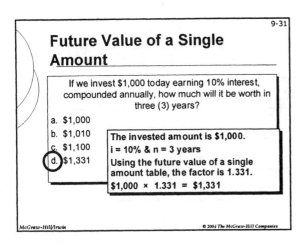

Future Value of a Single Amount

If we invest $1,000 today earning 10% interest, compounded annually, how much will it be worth in three (3) years?

a. $1,000
b. $1,010
c. $1,100
d. $1,331

The invested amount is $1,000.
i = 10% & n = 3 years
Using the future value of a single amount table, the factor is 1.331.
$1,000 × 1.331 = $1,331

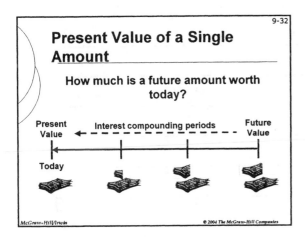

Present Value of a Single Amount

How much is a future amount worth today?

Present Value ← Interest compounding periods ─ ─ ─ ─ Future Value

Today

Present Value of a Single Amount

How much do we need to invest today at 10% interest, compounded annually, if we need $1,331 in three (3) years?

a. $1,000.00
b. $ 990.00
c. $ 751.30
d. $ 970.00

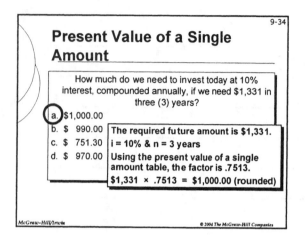

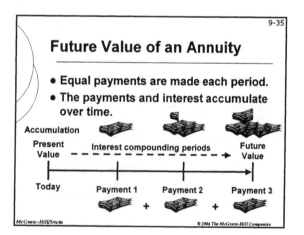

Future Value of an Annuity

If we invest $1,000 each year at interest of 10%, compounded annually, how much will we have at the end of three years?

a. $3,000
b. $3,090
c. $3,300
d. $3,310

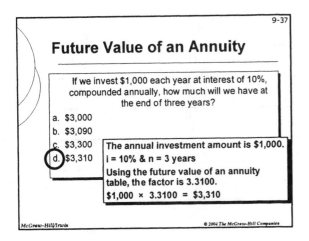

Future Value of an Annuity

If we invest $1,000 each year at interest of 10%, compounded annually, how much will we have at the end of three years?

a. $3,000
b. $3,090
c. $3,300
d. $3,310

The annual investment amount is $1,000.
i = 10% & n = 3 years
Using the future value of an annuity table, the factor is 3.3100.
$1,000 × 3.3100 = $3,310

McGraw-Hill/Irwin   © 2004 The McGraw-Hill Companies

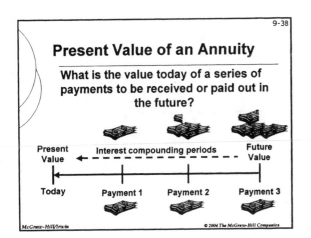

Present Value of an Annuity

What is the value today of a series of payments to be received or paid out in the future?

Present Value ← Interest compounding periods - - Future Value

Today   Payment 1   Payment 2   Payment 3

McGraw-Hill/Irwin   © 2004 The McGraw-Hill Companies

Present Value of an Annuity

What is the present value of receiving $1,000 each year for three years at interest of 10%, compounded annually?

a. $3,000.00
b. $2,910.00
c. $2,700.00
d. $2,486.90

McGraw-Hill/Irwin   © 2004 The McGraw-Hill Companies

Present Value of an Annuity

What is the present value of receiving $1,000 each year for three years at interest of 10%, compounded annually?

a. $3,000.00
b. $2,910.00
c. $2,700.00
d. $2,486.90

The annual receipt amount is $1,000.

i = 10% & n = 3 years

Using the present value of an annuity table, the factor is 2.4869.

$1,000 × 2.4869 = $2,486.90

McGraw-Hill/Irwin
© 2004 The McGraw-Hill Companies

End of Chapter 9

McGraw-Hill/Irwin
© 2004 The McGraw-Hill Companies

Chapter 10

Reporting and Interpreting Bonds

Understanding the Business

The mixture of debt and equity used to finance a company's operations is called the capital structure:

Debt - funds from creditors

Equity - funds from owners

McGraw-Hill/Irwin © 2004 The McGraw-Hill Companies

Understanding the Business: Capital Structure - Bonds

Significant debt needs of a company are often filled by issuing bonds.

Bonds   Cash

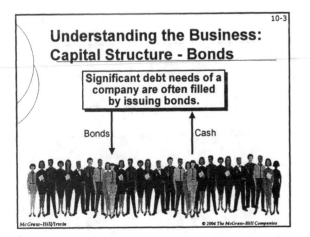

McGraw-Hill/Irwin © 2004 The McGraw-Hill Companies

10-4

Understanding the Business

Bonds can be traded on established exchanges that provide liquidity to bondholders.

As liquidity increases . . .

. . . Cost of borrowing decreases.

McGraw-Hill/Irwin

© 2004 The McGraw-Hill Companies

10-5

Understanding the Business

Advantages of bonds:

- Bonds are debt, not equity, so the ownership and control of the company are not diluted.
- Interest expense is tax-deductible.
- The low interest rates on bonds allow for positive financial leverage.

McGraw-Hill/Irwin

© 2004 The McGraw-Hill Companies

10-6

Understanding the Business

Disadvantages of bonds:

- Risk of bankruptcy; the debt must be paid back regularly, or creditors will force legal action.
- Negative impact on cash flows.

McGraw-Hill/Irwin

© 2004 The McGraw-Hill Companies

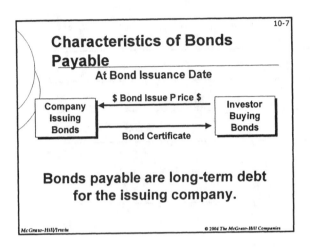

Characteristics of Bonds Payable

At Bond Issuance Date

$ Bond Issue Price $

Company Issuing Bonds → Investor Buying Bonds

Bond Certificate

Bonds payable are long-term debt for the issuing company.

McGraw-Hill/Irwin © 2004 The McGraw-Hill Companies

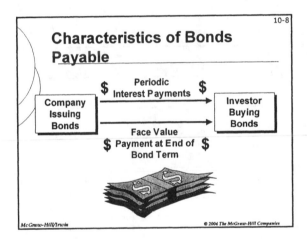

Characteristics of Bonds Payable

$ Periodic Interest Payments $

Company Issuing Bonds → Investor Buying Bonds

$ Face Value Payment at End of Bond Term $

McGraw-Hill/Irwin © 2004 The McGraw-Hill Companies

Characteristics of Bonds Payable

Face Value $1,000	Interest 10%
	6/30 & 12/31

BOND PAYABLE

Bond Date 1/1/01	Maturity Date 1/1/10

1. Face Value = Maturity or Par Value, Principal
2. Maturity Date
3. Stated Interest Rate   Other Factors:
4. Interest Payment Dates   6. Market Interest Rate
5. Bond Date   7. Issue Date

McGraw-Hill/Irwin © 2004 The McGraw-Hill Companies

Characteristics of Bonds Payable

- When issuing bonds, potential buyers of the bonds are given a prospectus.
- The company's bonds are issued to investors through an underwriter.
- The trustee makes sure the issuer fulfills all of the provisions of the bond indenture.

McGraw-Hill/Irwin © 2004 The McGraw-Hill Companies

Bond Classifications

- Debenture bonds
  - Not secured with the pledge of a specific asset.
- Callable bonds
  - May be retired and repaid (called) at any time at the option of the issuer.
- Redeemable bonds
  - May be turned in at any time for repayment at the option of the bondholder.
- Convertible bonds
  - May be exchanged for other securities of the issuer (usually shares of common stock) at the option of the bondholder.

McGraw-Hill/Irwin © 2004 The McGraw-Hill Companies

Key Ratio Analysis

The debt-equity ratio is an important measure of the balance between debt and equity.

Debt/equity ratio = Total liabilities / Owners' equity

High debt-equity ratios indicate more leverage and risk.

McGraw-Hill/Irwin © 2004 The McGraw-Hill Companies

Reporting Bond Transactions

When a company issues bonds, it specifies two cash flows related to the transaction: the original amount borrowed and the interest payments that will be made during the life of the bond.

Assume Dino Oil issues $100,000 in bonds at par on May 1, 2004. What journal entry should be made?

Date	Description	Debit	Credit
May 1	Cash	100,000	
	Bonds Payable		100,000

McGraw-Hill/Irwin © 2004 The McGraw-Hill Companies

Reporting Bond Transactions

Periodically, interest must be accrued and recorded. The interest payment is determined by multiplying the bond interest rate times the face amount of the bond.

Assume Dino Oil issues $100,000 in bonds at par on May 1, 2004. The bonds pay 8% interest annually. What journal entry should be made on April 30, 2005?

Date	Description	Debit	Credit
Apr 30	Interest Expense	8,000	
	Interest Payable		8,000

McGraw-Hill/Irwin © 2004 The McGraw-Hill Companies

Measuring Bonds Payable and Interest Expense

The issue price of the bond is determined by the market, based on the time value of money.

Present Value of the Principal (a single payment)
+ Present Value of the Interest Payments (an annuity)
= Issue Price of the Bond

The interest rate used to compute the present value is the market interest rate.

McGraw-Hill/Irwin © 2004 The McGraw-Hill Companies

Measuring Bonds Payable and Interest Expense

The stated rate is only used to compute the periodic interest payments.

Interest = Principal × Stated Rate × Time

Key Ratio Analysis

$$\text{Times Interest Earned} = \frac{\text{Net income} + \text{Interest expense} + \text{Income tax expense}}{\text{Interest expense}}$$

The ratio shows the amount of resources generated for each dollar of interest expense. In general, a high ratio is viewed more favorable than a low ratio.

Bond Premium and Discounts

Interest Rates		Bond Price		Accounting for the Difference
Stated Rate =	Market Rate	Bond Price =	Par Value of the Bond	There is no difference to account for
Stated Rate <	Market Rate	Bond Price <	Par Value of the Bond	The difference is accounted for as a bond discount
Stated Rate >	Market Rate	Bond Price >	Par Value of the Bond	The difference is accounted for as a bond premium

Computing Bond Prices

On January 1, 2003, Harrah's issues
$100,000 in bonds having a stated rate of
10% annually. The bonds mature in 10
years and interest is paid semiannually.
The market rate is 12% annually.

**Are Harrah's bonds issued at
par, at a discount, or at a
premium?**

McGraw-Hill/Irwin   © 2004 The McGraw-Hill Companies

Computing Bond Prices

On January 1, 2003, Harrah's issues
$100,000 in bonds having a stated rate of
10% annually. The bonds mature in 10
years and interest is paid semiannually.
The market rate is 12% annually.

Interest Rates		Bond Price		Accounting for the Difference
Stated Rate	< Market Rate	Bond Price	< Par Value of the Bond	The difference is accounted for as a bond discount.

McGraw-Hill/Irwin   © 2004 The McGraw-Hill Companies

Computing Bond Prices

On January 1, 2003, Harrah's issues
$100,000 in bonds having a stated rate of
10% annually. The bonds mature in 10
years and interest is paid semiannually.
The market rate is 12% annually.

**Compute the issue price of
Harrah's bonds.**

McGraw-Hill/Irwin   © 2004 The McGraw-Hill Companies

Computing Bond Prices

1. Compute the present value of the principal.

Present Value
Single Amount = Principal × Factor

Use the present value of a single amount table to find the appropriate factor.

McGraw-Hill/Irwin   © 2004 The McGraw-Hill Companies

Computing Bond Prices

1. Compute the present value of the principal.

Present Value
Single Amount = Principal × Factor, i=6.0%

Use the market rate of 12% to determine present value. Interest is paid semiannually, so the rate is i = 6% (12% ÷ 2 interest periods per year).

McGraw-Hill/Irwin   © 2004 The McGraw-Hill Companies

Computing Bond Prices

1. Compute the present value of the principal.

Present Value
Single Amount = Principal × Factor, i=6.0%, n=20

Though the maturity period is 10 years, there are 2 interest periods per year. For the present value computation, use n=20 (10 years × 2 periods per year).

McGraw-Hill/Irwin   © 2004 The McGraw-Hill Companies

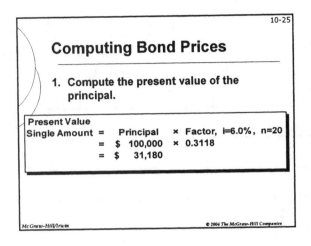

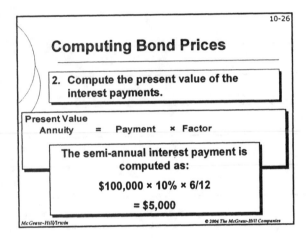

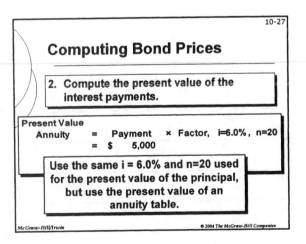

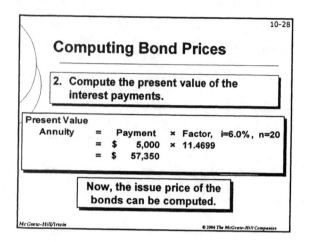

Computing Bond Prices

2. Compute the present value of the interest payments.

Present Value
Annuity   =   Payment   × Factor,   i=6.0%, n=20
        = $ 5,000   ×   11.4699
        = $ 57,350

Now, the issue price of the bonds can be computed.

McGraw-Hill/Irwin   © 2004 The McGraw-Hill Companies

Computing Bond Prices

3. Compute the issue price of the bonds.

    $ 31,180   Present Value of the Principal
+   57,350   Present Value of the Interest
= $ 88,530   Present Value of the Bonds

McGraw-Hill/Irwin   © 2004 The McGraw-Hill Companies

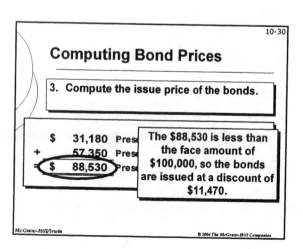

Computing Bond Prices

3. Compute the issue price of the bonds.

    $ 31,180   Pres
+   57,350   Pres
= $ 88,530   Pres

The $88,530 is less than the face amount of $100,000, so the bonds are issued at a discount of $11,470.

McGraw-Hill/Irwin   © 2004 The McGraw-Hill Companies

Recording Bonds
Issued at a Discount

4. Prepare the journal entry to record the issuance of the bonds.

GENERAL JOURNAL			Page	97
Date	Description		Debit	Credit
Jan	1	Cash	88,530	
		Discount on Bonds Payable	11,470	
		Bonds Payable		100,000
		to record issuance of bonds		

This is a contra-liability account and appears in the liability section of the balance sheet.

McGraw-Hill/Irwin   © 2004 The McGraw-Hill Companies

Bonds Issued at a Discount
Financial Statement Presentation

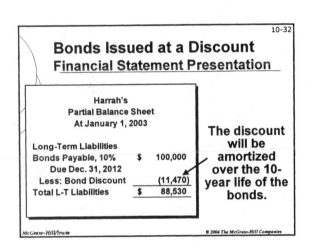

Harrah's
Partial Balance Sheet
At January 1, 2003

Long-Term Liabilities
Bonds Payable, 10% $ 100,000
   Due Dec. 31, 2012
   Less: Bond Discount   (11,470)
Total L-T Liabilities $ 88,530

The discount will be amortized over the 10-year life of the bonds.

McGraw-Hill/Irwin   © 2004 The McGraw-Hill Companies

Bonds Issued at a Discount
Financial Statement Presentation

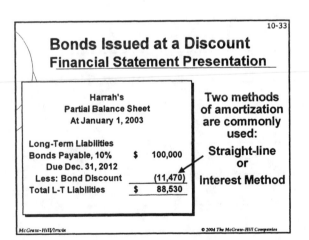

Harrah's
Partial Balance Sheet
At January 1, 2003

Long-Term Liabilities
Bonds Payable, 10% $ 100,000
   Due Dec. 31, 2012
   Less: Bond Discount   (11,470)
Total L-T Liabilities $ 88,530

Two methods of amortization are commonly used:

Straight-line or Interest Method

McGraw-Hill/Irwin   © 2004 The McGraw-Hill Companies

10-34

Straight-Line Amortization of Bond Discount

- Identify the amount of the bond discount.
- Divide the bond discount by the number of interest periods.
- Include the discount amortization amount as part of the periodic interest expense entry.
  - The discount will be reduced to zero by the maturity date.

McGraw-Hill/Irwin   © 2004 The McGraw-Hill Companies

10-35

Straight-Line Amortization of Bond Discount

Harrah's issued their bonds on Jan. 1, 2003. The discount was $11,470. The bonds have a 10-year maturity and $5,000 interest is paid semiannually.

Compute the periodic discount amortization using the straight-line method.

Discount Amortization	=	Total Discount	+	Number of Interest Periods

McGraw-Hill/Irwin   © 2004 The McGraw-Hill Companies

10-36

Straight-Line Amortization of Bond Discount

Harrah's issued their bonds on Jan. 1, 2003. The discount was $11,470. The bonds have a 10-year maturity and $5,000 interest is paid semiannually.

Compute the periodic discount amortization using the straight-line method.

Discount Amortization	=	Total Discount	+	Number of Interest Periods
	=	$ 11,470	+	20
	=	$ 574		per period (rounded)

McGraw-Hill/Irwin   © 2004 The McGraw-Hill Companies

Straight-Line Amortization of Bond Discount

Prepare the journal entry to record the payment of interest and the discount amortization for the six months ending on June 30, 2003.

Date		Description	Debit	Credit
Jun	30	Interest Expense	5,574	
		Discount on Bonds Payable		574
		Cash		5,000
		to record payment of interest		

GENERAL JOURNAL — Page 123

McGraw-Hill/Irwin © 2004 The McGraw-Hill Companies

Bonds Issued at a Discount
Financial Statement Presentation

Harrah's
Partial Balance Sheet
At June 30, 2003

Long-Term Liabilities
Bonds Payable, 10% $ 100,000
  Due Dec. 31, 2012
  Less: Bond Discount   (10,896)
Total L-T Liabilities $ 89,104

As the discount is amortized, the carrying amount of the bonds increases.

McGraw-Hill/Irwin © 2004 The McGraw-Hill Companies

Zero Coupon Bonds

- Zero coupon bonds do not pay periodic interest.
- Because there is no interest annuity . . .

PV of the Principal = Issue Price of the Bonds

- This is called a deep discount bond.

McGraw-Hill/Irwin © 2004 The McGraw-Hill Companies

Slide 10-40

Issuing Bonds at a Premium

Interest Rates		Bond Price		Accounting for the Difference
Stated Rate	= Market Rate	Bond Price	= Par Value of the Bond	There is no difference to account for
Stated Rate	< Market Rate	Bond Price	< Par Value of the Bond	The difference is accounted for as a bond discount
Stated Rate	> Market Rate	Bond Price	> Par Value of the Bond	The difference is accounted for as a bond premium

McGraw-Hill/Irwin   © 2004 The McGraw-Hill Companies

Slide 10-41

Issuing Bonds at a Premium

On January 1, 2003, Harrah's issues $100,000 in bonds having a stated rate of 10% annually. The bonds mature in 10 years and interest is paid semiannually. The market rate is 8% annually.

Are Harrah's bonds issued at par, at a discount, or at a premium?

McGraw-Hill/Irwin   © 2004 The McGraw-Hill Companies

Slide 10-42

Issuing Bonds at a Premium

On January 1, 2003, Harrah's issues $100,000 in bonds having a stated rate of 10% annually. The bonds mature in 10 years and interest is paid semiannually. The market rate is 8% annually.

Interest Rates		Bond Price		Accounting for the Difference
Stated Rate	> Market Rate	Bond Price	> Par Value of the Bond	The difference is accounted for as a bond premium.

Let's compute the issue price of the bonds.

McGraw-Hill/Irwin   © 2004 The McGraw-Hill Companies

Issuing Bonds at a Premium

1. Compute the present value of the principal.

Present Value
Single Amount = Principal × Factor

Use the present value of a single amount table to find the appropriate factor.

McGraw-Hill/Irwin   © 2004 The McGraw-Hill Companies

Issuing Bonds at a Premium

1. Compute the present value of the principal.

Present Value
Single Amount = Principal × Factor, i=4.0%

Use the market rate of 8% to determine present value. Interest is paid semiannually, so the rate is i = 4.0% (8% ÷ 2 interest periods per year).

McGraw-Hill/Irwin   © 2004 The McGraw-Hill Companies

Issuing Bonds at a Premium

1. Compute the present value of the principal.

Present Value
Single Amount = Principal × Factor, i=4.0%, n=20

The maturity period is 10 years, there are 2 interest periods per year. For the present value computation, use n=20 (10 years × 2 periods).

McGraw-Hill/Irwin   © 2004 The McGraw-Hill Companies

Issuing Bonds at a Premium

1. Compute the present value of the principal.

Present Value
Single Amount =   Principal   × Factor, i=4.0%, n=20
        = $ 100,000 × 0.4564
        = $ 45,640

Next, we compute the present value of the interest payments.

McGraw-Hill/Irwin   © 2004 The McGraw-Hill Companies

Issuing Bonds at a Premium

2. Compute the present value of the interest payments.

Present Value
  Annuity   =   Payment   × Factor

The semiannual interest payment is computed as:

$100,000 × 10% × 6/12

= $5,000

McGraw-Hill/Irwin   © 2004 The McGraw-Hill Companies

Issuing Bonds at a Premium

2. Compute the present value of the interest payments.

Present Value
  Annuity   =   Payment   × Factor, i=4.0%, n=20
        = $ 5,000

Use the same i=4.0% and n=20 that were used to compute the present value of the principal. Now, however, the factor comes from the present value of an annuity table.

McGraw-Hill/Irwin   © 2004 The McGraw-Hill Companies

Issuing Bonds at a Premium

2. Compute the present value of the interest payments.

Present Value
Annuity = Payment × Factor, i=4.0%, n=20
= $ 5,000 × 13.5903
= $ 67,952

Now, the issue price of the bonds can be computed.

McGraw-Hill/Irwin © 2004 The McGraw-Hill Companies

Issuing Bonds at a Premium

3. Compute the present value of the interest payments.

$45,640 Present Value of the Principal
+ 67,952 Present Value of the Interest
= $113,592 Present Value of the Bonds

The $113,592 is greater than the face amount of $100,000, so the bonds are issued at a premium of $13,592.

McGraw-Hill/Irwin © 2004 The McGraw-Hill Companies

Issuing Bonds at a Premium

4. Prepare the journal entry to record the issuance of the bonds at a premium.

GENERAL JOURNAL		Page	97
Date	Description	Debit	Credit
Jan 1	Cash	113,592	
	Bonds Payable		100,000
	Premium on Bonds Payable		3,592

This is called an adjunct account and appears in the liability section.

McGraw-Hill/Irwin © 2004 The McGraw-Hill Companies

Bonds Issued at a Premium
Financial Statement Presentation

Harrah's
Partial Balance Sheet
At January 1, 2003

Long-Term Liabilities
Bonds Payable, 10% $ 100,000
Due Dec. 31, 2012
Add: Bond Premium   13,592
Total L-T Liabilities $ 113,592

The premium will be amortized over the 10-year life of the bonds.

McGraw-Hill/Irwin   © 2004 The McGraw-Hill Companies

Effective-Interest Amortization of Bond Discounts and Premiums

The effective-interest method computes interest as:

Bond Carrying Value × Market Rate

Principal amount of the bonds less any unamortized discount or plus any unamortized premium.

McGraw-Hill/Irwin   © 2004 The McGraw-Hill Companies

Effective-Interest Amortization of Bond Discounts and Premiums

The effective-interest method computes interest as:

Bond Carrying Value × Market Rate

This is the same market rate used to determine the present value of the bond.

McGraw-Hill/Irwin   © 2004 The McGraw-Hill Companies

Effective-Interest Method

Recall our first example of Harrah's. On Jan. 1, 2003, the company issues $100,000 in bonds having a stated rate of 10% annually. The bonds mature in 10 years and interest is paid semiannually. The market rate is 12% annually.

	GENERAL JOURNAL	Page	97
Date	Description	Debit	Credit
Jan 1	Cash	88,530	
	Discount on Bonds Payable	11,470	
	Bonds Payable		100,000
	to record issuance of bonds		

McGraw-Hill/Irwin © 2004 The McGraw-Hill Companies

Effective-Interest Method

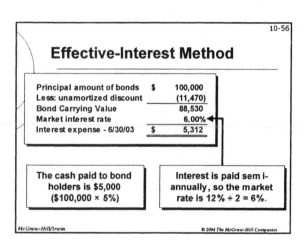

Principal amount of bonds	$	100,000
Less: unamortized discount		(11,470)
Bond Carrying Value		88,530
Market interest rate		6.00%
Interest expense - 6/30/03	$	5,312

The cash paid to bond holders is $5,000 ($100,000 × 5%)

Interest is paid semi-annually, so the market rate is 12% ÷ 2 = 6%.

McGraw-Hill/Irwin © 2004 The McGraw-Hill Companies

Effective-Interest Method

The journal entry to record the first interest payment is:

	GENERAL JOURNAL	Page	123
Date	Description	Debit	Credit
Jun 30	Interest Expense	5,312	
	Discount on Bonds Payable		312
	Cash		5,000
	to record issuance of bonds		

McGraw-Hill/Irwin © 2004 The McGraw-Hill Companies

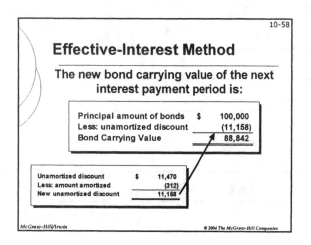

10-58

Effective-Interest Method

The new bond carrying value of the next
interest payment period is:

Principal amount of bonds	$	100,000
Less: unamortized discount		(11,158)
Bond Carrying Value		88,842

Unamortized discount	$	11,470
Less: amount amortized		(312)
New unamortized discount		11,158

McGraw-Hill/Irwin · © 2004 The McGraw-Hill Companies

10-59

Understanding Alternative Amortization Methods

- Effective-interest method of amortization is preferred by GAAP.
- Straight-line amortization may be used if it is not materially different from effective interest amortization.

McGraw-Hill/Irwin · © 2004 The McGraw-Hill Companies

10-60

Early Retirement of Debt

- Occasionally, the issuing company will call (repay early) some or all of its bonds.
- Gains/losses incurred as a result of retiring bonds should be reported as an extraordinary item on the income statement.

McGraw-Hill/Irwin · © 2004 The McGraw-Hill Companies

10-61

Focus on Cash Flows

Financing activities –
- ❖ Issuance of bonds (a cash inflow)
- ❖ Retire debt (a cash outflow)
- ❖ Repay bond principal at maturity (a cash outflow)

McGraw-Hill/Irwin
© 2004 The McGraw-Hill Companies

10-62

End of Chapter 10

McGraw-Hill/Irwin
© 2004 The McGraw-Hill Companies

Chapter 11

Reporting and Interpreting
Owners' Equity

Understanding The Business

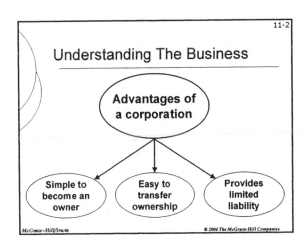

Understanding The Business

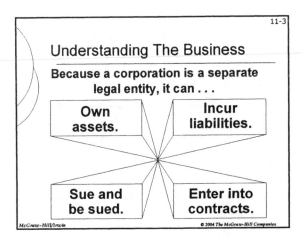

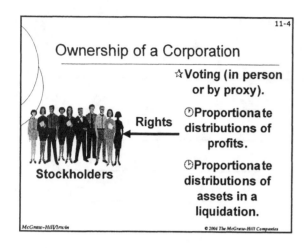

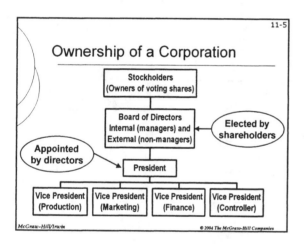

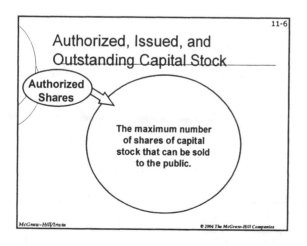

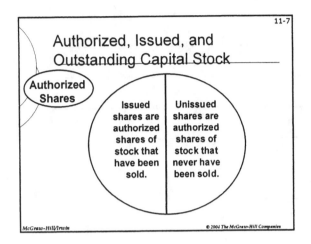

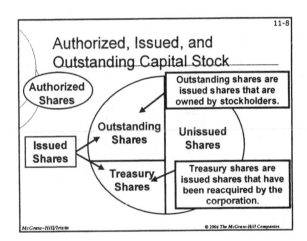

Earnings Per share (EPS)

$$EPS = \frac{Income}{Average\ Number\ of\ Shares\ Outstanding}$$

Outback's income for 2000 is $141,000,000 and the average number of shares outstanding is 77,500,000.

Earnings per share is probably the single most widely watched financial ratio.

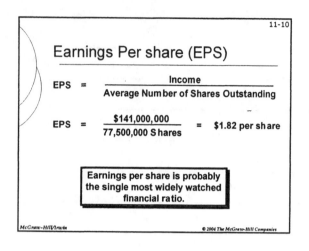

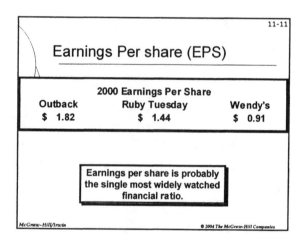

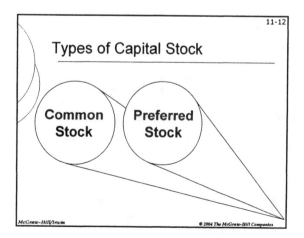

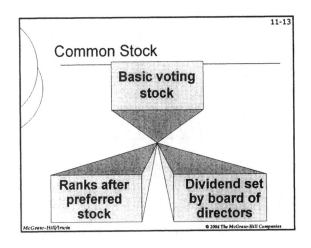

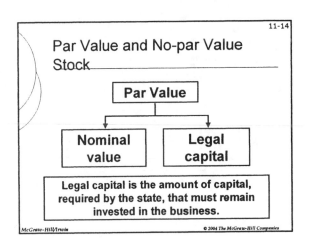

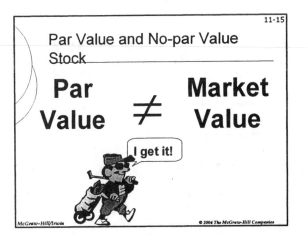

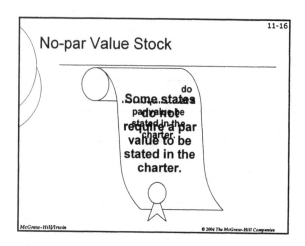

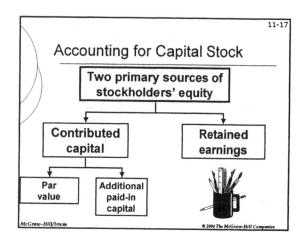

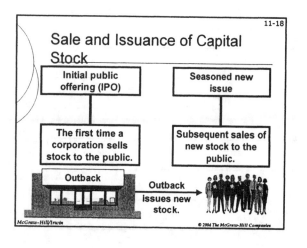

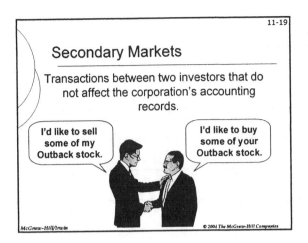

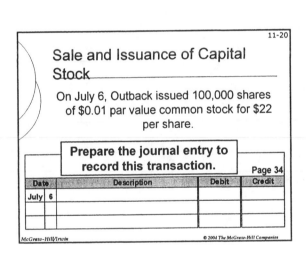

Sale and Issuance of Capital Stock

On July 6, Outback issued 100,000 shares of $0.01 par value common stock for $22 per share.

100,000 shares × $0.01 par value = $1,000

100,000 shares × $22 per share = $2,200,000		Page 34	
Date	Description	Debit	Credit
July 6	Cash	2,200,000	
	Common Stock		1,000
	Capital In Excess of Par Value		2,199,000

McGraw-Hill/Irwin © 2004 The McGraw-Hill Companies

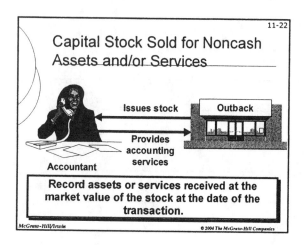

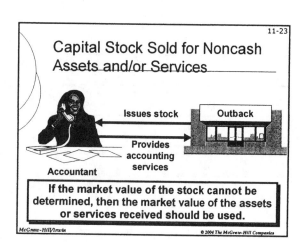

Capital Stock Sold for Noncash Assets and/or Services

On March 14, Outback issued 10,000 shares of its $0.01 par value common stock to the Rose Law firms. The stock was selling for $15 per share.

Prepare the journal entry to record this transaction.

Date					
Mar. 14					

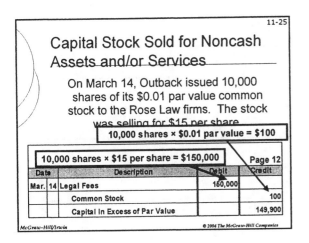

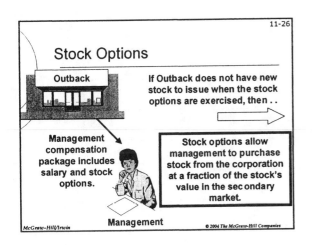

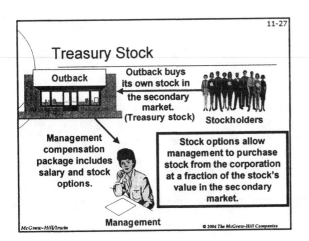

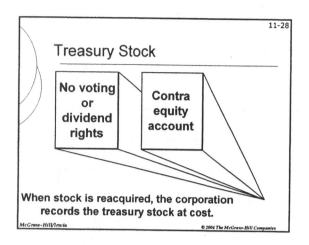

Treasury Stock

11-28

No voting or dividend rights

Contra equity account

When stock is reacquired, the corporation records the treasury stock at cost.

McGraw-Hill/Irwin © 2004 The McGraw-Hill Companies

Treasury Stock

11-29

On May 1, Outback reacquired 100,000 shares of its common stock at $20 per share.

The journal entry for May 1 is . . . .

GENERAL JOURNAL			Page 27
Date	Description	Debit	Credit
May 1	Treasury Stock	2,000,000	
	Cash		2,000,000
	100,000 shares × $20 = $2,000,000		

McGraw-Hill/Irwin © 2004 The McGraw-Hill Companies

Treasury Stock

11-30

On December 3, Outback reissued 10,000 shares of the treasury stock at $30 per share.

The journal entry for December 3 is . . .

10,000 shares × $20 cost = $200,000

10,000 shares × $30 = $300,000

			Page 68
Date	Description	Debit	Credit
Dec. 3	Cash	300,000	
	Treasury Stock		200,000
	Capital in Excess of Par		100,000

McGraw-Hill/Irwin © 2004 The McGraw-Hill Companies

Accounting for Cash Dividends

Declared by board of directors.	Not legally required.

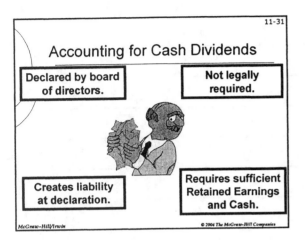

Creates liability at declaration.	Requires sufficient Retained Earnings and Cash.

McGraw-Hill/Irwin   © 2004 The McGraw-Hill Companies

Dividend Dates

Declaration date
- Board of directors declares the dividend.
- Record a liability.

GENERAL JOURNAL				Page 12
Date	Description	Post. Ref.	Debit	Credit
	Retained Earnings		XXX	
	Dividends Payable			XXX

McGraw-Hill/Irwin   © 2004 The McGraw-Hill Companies

Dividend Dates

Date of Record
- Stockholders holding shares on this date will receive the dividend. (No entry)

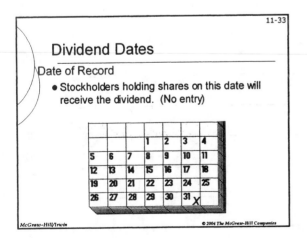

McGraw-Hill/Irwin   © 2004 The McGraw-Hill Companies

Dividend Dates

Date of Payment
- Record the dividend payment to stockholders.

	GENERAL JOURNAL			Page 12
Date	Description	Post. Ref.	Debit	Credit
	Dividends Payable		XXX	
	Cash			XXX

Dividend Yield Ratio

$$\text{Dividend Yield} = \frac{\text{Dividends Per Share}}{\text{Market Price Per Share}}$$

Outback does not pay a cash dividend. The 2000 market price is $27.

This ratio is often used to compare the dividend-paying performance of different investment alternatives.

Dividend Yield Ratio

$$\text{Dividend Yield} = \frac{\text{Dividends Per Share}}{\text{Market Price Per Share}}$$

$$\text{Dividend Yield} = \frac{\$0.00}{\$27.00} = 0.0\%$$

This ratio is often used to compare the dividend-paying performance of different investment alternatives.

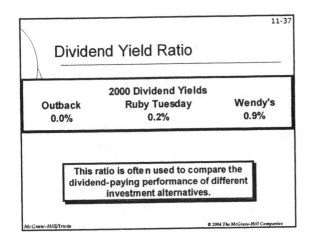

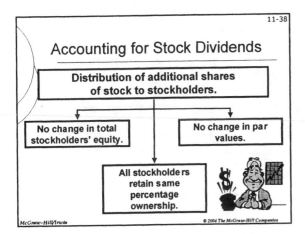

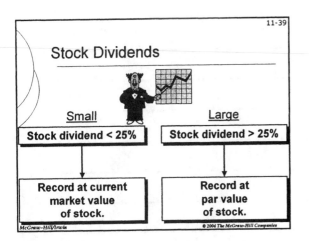

Stock Splits

Distributions of 100% or more of stock to stockholders.

Ice Cream Parlor

Banana Splits On Sale Now

Stock Splits

Assume that a corporation had 5,000 shares of $1 par value common stock outstanding before a 2–for–1 stock split.

	Before Split	After Split
Common Stock Shares	5,000	
Par Value per Share	$ 1.00	
Total Par Value	$ 5,000	

Stock Splits

Assume that a corporation had 5,000 shares of $1 par value common stock outstanding before a 2–for–1 stock split.

	Before Split	After Split	
Common Stock Shares	5,000	10,000	Increase
Par Value per Share	$ 1.00	$ 0.50	Decrease
Total Par Value	$ 5,000	$ 5,000	No Change

Preferred Stock

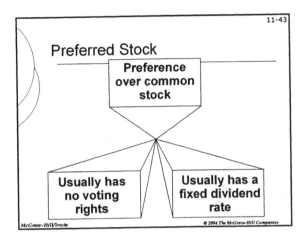

Preference over common stock

Usually has no voting rights

Usually has a fixed dividend rate

McGraw-Hill/Irwin © 2004 The McGraw-Hill Companies

_____

_____

_____

_____

_____

_____

_____

Dividends on Preferred Stock

☆ Current Dividend Preference: The current preferred dividends must be paid before paying any dividends to common stock.

⏲ Cumulative Dividend Preference: Any unpaid dividends from previous years (dividends in arrears) must be paid before common dividends are paid.

McGraw-Hill/Irwin © 2004 The McGraw-Hill Companies

_____

_____

_____

_____

_____

_____

_____

_____

Dividends on Preferred Stock

If the preferred stock is noncumulative, any dividends not declared in previous years are lost permanently.

McGraw-Hill/Irwin © 2004 The McGraw-Hill Companies

_____

_____

_____

_____

_____

_____

_____

Dividends on Preferred Stock

Kites, Inc. has the following stock outstanding:

Common stock: $1 par, 100,000 shares
Preferred stock: 3%, $100 par, cumulative, 5,000 shares
Preferred stock: 6%, $50 par, noncumulative, 3,000 shares

Dividends were not paid last year. In the current year, the board of directors declared dividends of $50,000.

How much will each class of stock receive?

Dividends on Preferred Stock

Total dividend declared	**$ 50,000**
Preferred stock (cumulative)	
Remainder	
Preferred stock (noncumulative)	
Remainder	
Common stock	
Remainder	

Dividends on Preferred Stock

Total dividend declared		**$ 50,000**
Preferred stock (cumulative)		
Arrearage ($100 par × 3% × 5,000 shares)	$ 15,000	
Current Yr. ($100 par × 3% × 5,000 shares)	15,000	30,000
Remainder		$ 20,000
Preferred stock (noncumulative)		
Remainder		
Common stock		
Remainder		

Dividends on Preferred Stock

Total dividend declared		$ 50,000
Preferred stock (cumulative)		
Arrearage ($100 par × 3% × 5,000 shares)	$ 15,000	
Current Yr. ($100 par × 3% × 5,000 shares)	15,000	30,000
Remainder		$ 20,000
Preferred stock (noncumulative)		
Current Yr. ($50 par × 6% × 3,000 shares)		9,000
Remainder		$ 11,000
Common stock		
Remainder		

McGraw-Hill/Irwin © 2004 The McGraw-Hill Companies

Dividends on Preferred Stock

Total dividend declared		$ 50,000
Preferred stock (cumulative)		
Arrearage ($100 par × 3% × 5,000 shares)	$ 15,000	
Current Yr. ($100 par × 3% × 5,000 shares)	15,000	30,000
Remainder		$ 20,000
Preferred stock (noncumulative)		
Current Yr. ($50 par × 6% × 3,000 shares)		9,000
Remainder		$ 11,000
Common stock		
Current Yr. ($11,000 Remainder)		11,000
Remainder		$ 0

McGraw-Hill/Irwin © 2004 The McGraw-Hill Companies

Dividends

On June 1, 2003, a corporation's board of directors declared a dividend for the 2,500 shares of its $100 par value, 8% preferred stock. The dividend will be paid on July 15. Which of the following will be included in the July 15 entry?

a. Debit Retained Earnings $20,000.

b. Debit Dividends Payable $20,000.

c. Credit Dividends Payable $20,000.

d. Credit Preferred Stock $20,000.

McGraw-Hill/Irwin © 2004 The McGraw-Hill Companies

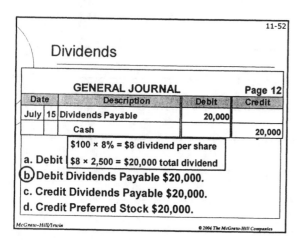

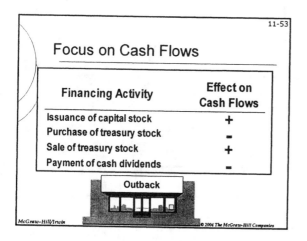

Accounting and Reporting for Three Types of Businesses

	Corporation (Stockholders' Equity)	Sole Proprietorship (Owner's Equity)	Partnership (Partners' Equity)
Equity Accounts	Capital Stock	Doe, Capital	Able, Capital Baker, Capital
	Contributed Capital in Excess of Par	Not used	Not used
	Retained Earnings	Not used	Not used
Distributions to Owners	Dividends Paid	Doe, Drawings	Able, Drawings Baker, Drawings
Closing Entries	Income Summary (closed to Retained Earnings)	Income Summary (closed to Doe, Capital)	Income Summary (closed to Able, Capital and Baker, Capital)
Income Statement	Revenues, expenses, gains and losses	Same	Same
Balance Sheet	Assets and liabilities	Same	Same

Chapter 12

Reporting and Interpreting Investments in Other Corporations

Understanding the Business

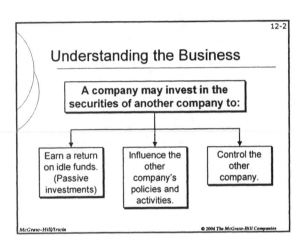

A company may invest in the securities of another company to:

| Earn a return on idle funds. (Passive investments) | Influence the other company's policies and activities. | Control the other company. |

Types of Investments

Passive investments are made to earn a high rate of return on funds that may be needed for future purposes.

Investments in debt securities are always considered passive investments.

%

Types of Investments

Passive investments are made to earn a high rate of return on funds that may be needed for future purposes.

Equity security investments are presumed passive if the investing company owns less than **20%** of the outstanding voting shares.

Investor is not interested in controlling or influencing other company.

McGraw-Hill/Irwin   © 2004 The McGraw-Hill Companies

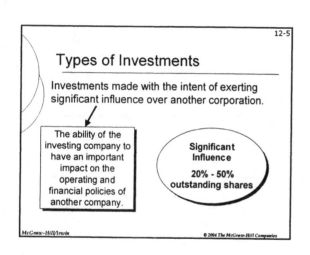

Types of Investments

Investments made with the intent of exerting significant influence over another corporation.

The ability of the investing company to have an important impact on the operating and financial policies of another company.

Significant Influence

20% - 50% outstanding shares

McGraw-Hill/Irwin   © 2004 The McGraw-Hill Companies

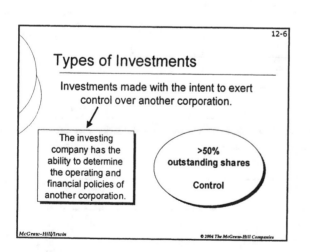

Types of Investments

Investments made with the intent to exert control over another corporation.

The investing company has the ability to determine the operating and financial policies of another corporation.

>50% outstanding shares

Control

McGraw-Hill/Irwin   © 2004 The McGraw-Hill Companies

Types of Investments and Accounting Methods

The accounting method depends on the type of security and the level of ownership (influence).

Investment Category		Measuring and Reporting Method
Debt	Passive, Held-to-maturity	Amortized cost
Stock	Passive	Market value
Stock	Significant influence	Equity
Stock	Control	Consolidated statement

McGraw-Hill/Irwin © 2004 The McGraw-Hill Companies

Debt Held To Maturity: Amortized Cost Method

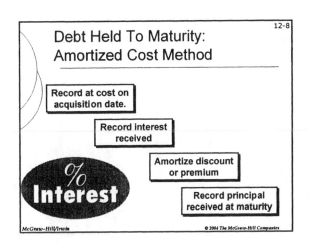

Record at cost on acquisition date.

Record interest received

Amortize discount or premium

Record principal received at maturity

% Interest

McGraw-Hill/Irwin © 2004 The McGraw-Hill Companies

Passive Stock Investments: The Market Value Method

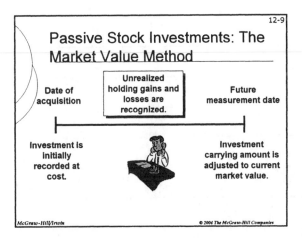

Date of acquisition

Unrealized holding gains and losses are recognized.

Future measurement date

Investment is initially recorded at cost.

Investment carrying amount is adjusted to current market value.

McGraw-Hill/Irwin © 2004 The McGraw-Hill Companies

Classifying Passive Stock Investments

		Effect of Unrealized Holding Gains and Losses On . . .		
Type of Investment	Definition	Investment Account	Equity	Net Income
Trading Securities	Held primarily for resale.	Allowance Account	N/A	Reported on the Income Statement
Securities Available for Sale	Not held primarily for resale.	Allowance Account	Reported as part of equity	N/A

NOTE: Realized gains and losses go on the Income Statement.

McGraw-Hill/Irwin   © 2004 The McGraw-Hill Companies

Securities Available for Sale (SAS)

IFNews and Dow Jones both produce film. Dow Jones wants to acquire an ownership interest in IFNews.

On 1/05/03, Dow Jones acquires 10,000 of the 100,000 shares outstanding on the open market at a cost of $60 per share. Dow Jones has no influence over IFNews, and does not plan to sell the shares in the near future.

McGraw-Hill/Irwin   © 2004 The McGraw-Hill Companies

Securities Available for Sale (SAS)

Should the acquired shares be classified as Trading Securities or Securities Available for Sale?

Dow Jones does not plan to sell the shares, so they should be classified as Securities Available for Sale.

The journal entry to record the investment is . . . ⟹

McGraw-Hill/Irwin   © 2004 The McGraw-Hill Companies

Securities Available for Sale (SAS)

GENERAL JOURNAL			Page 39	
Date	Description		Debit	Credit
Jan. 5	Investment in SAS		600,000	
	Cash			600,000

Securities Available for Sale are classified as noncurrent assets.

Securities Available for Sale (SAS)

On July 2, Dow Jones receives a $10,000 dividend from IFNews. Prepare the journal entry to record the dividend.

GENERAL JOURNAL			Page 39	
Date	Description		Debit	Credit
July 2				

Securities Available for Sale (SAS)

On July 2, Dow Jones receives a $10,000 dividend from IFNews. Prepare the journal entry to record the dividend.

GENERAL JOURNAL			Page 39	
Date	Description		Debit	Credit
July 2	Cash		10,000	
	Investment Income			10,000

Securities Available for Sale (SAS)

By December 31, 2003, Dow Jones' fiscal year-end, the market value of IFNews' shares has dropped from $60 to $58 per share.

How much has Dow Jones' portfolio value changed?

10,000 shares × $2 / share = $20,000

The journal entry to recognize the change in market value is . . . ⟹

Securities Available for Sale (SAS)

GENERAL JOURNAL			Page 86	
Date		Description	Debit	Credit
Dec.	31	Net Unrealized Gains		
		and Losses - SAS	20,000	
		Allowance to Value at Market		20,000

The unrealized holding loss would be reported in the stockholders' equity section of Dow Jones' balance sheet.

Comparing Trading and Securities Available for Sale

Effects	Trading Securities	Securities Available for Sale
Income Statement Realized Gains	Sales Price > Cost	Same
Realized Losses	Sales Price < Cost	Same
Unrealized Gains and Losses	Adjust at Year-end	N/A
Balance Sheet Unrealized Gains and Losses	N/A	Adjust at Year-end

Investments For Significant Influence: Equity Method

Used when an investor can exert significant influence over an investee.

Investment Category		Measuring and Reporting Method
Debt	Passive, Held-to-maturity	Amortized cost
Stock	Passive	Market value
Stock	Significant influence	Equity
Stock	Control	Consolidated statement

It is presumed that the investment was made as a long-term investment.

Investments For Significant Influence: Equity Method

Date of acquisition

Unrealized holding gains and losses are not recognized.

Future measurement date

Investment is initially recorded at cost.

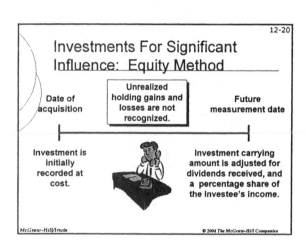

Investment carrying amount is adjusted for dividends received, and a percentage share of the investee's income.

Investments For Significant Influence: Equity Method

Adjusting Item	Effect on Investment Account
Dividends	Reduce investment for dividends received.
Investee Net Income	Increase investment by our proportionate share.
Investee Net Loss	Decrease investment by our proportionate share.

Investments For Significant Influence: Equity Method

On 1/1/03, TeleCom, Inc. acquires a 30% interest in Sports.com at a cost of $2,000,000. Prepare the journal entry to record TeleCom's investment.

GENERAL JOURNAL — Page 2

Date		Description	Debit	Credit
Jan.	1			

McGraw-Hill/Irwin © 2004 The McGraw-Hill Companies

Investments For Significant Influence: Equity Method

On 1/1/03, TeleCom, Inc. acquires a 30% interest in Sports.com at a cost of $2,000,000. Prepare the journal entry to record TeleCom's investment.

GENERAL JOURNAL — Page 2

Date		Description	Debit	Credit
Jan.	1	Investments in Associated Co.	2,000,000	
		Cash		2,000,000

McGraw-Hill/Irwin © 2004 The McGraw-Hill Companies

Investments For Significant Influence: Equity Method

On 3/31/03, Sports.com pays $200,000 in dividends, $60,000 (30%) of which goes to TeleCom. Record TeleCom's receipt of the dividend.

GENERAL JOURNAL — Page 46

Date		Description	Debit	Credit
Mar.	31			

McGraw-Hill/Irwin © 2004 The McGraw-Hill Companies

Investments For Significant Influence: Equity Method

On 3/31/03, Sports.com pays $200,000 in dividends, $60,000 (30%) of which goes to TeleCom. Record TeleCom's receipt of the dividend.

GENERAL JOURNAL — Page 46

Date		Description	Debit	Credit
Mar.	31	Cash	60,000	
		Investments in Associated Co.		60,000

Dividends are not revenue under the equity method. They are treated as a reduction of the investment account.

Investments For Significant Influence: Equity Method

Sports.com net income for the year ending 12/31/03 is $1,600,000. TeleCom's 30% share is $480,000. Record TeleCom's share of Sports.com's income.

GENERAL JOURNAL — Page 86

Date		Description	Debit	Credit
Dec.	31			

Investments For Significant Influence: Equity Method

Sports.com net income for the year ending 12/31/03 is $1,600,000. TeleCom's 30% share is $480,000. Record TeleCom's share of Sports.com's income.

GENERAL JOURNAL — Page 86

Date		Description	Debit	Credit
Dec.	31	Investment in Associated Co.	480,000	
		Equity in Investee Earnings		480,000

TeleCom credits Equity in Investee Earnings (an income statement account) for its share of Sports.com's earnings.

Focus on Cash Flows

Investing activities:
- Purchase of investment (cash outflow)
- Sale of investment (cash inflow)

Operating activities:
- Gain on sale of investment (subtract from net income)
- Loss on sale of investment (add to net income)
- Equity in earnings of investee (subtract from net income)
- Dividends from investee (add to net income)
- Unrealized holding gains trading securities (subtract from net income)
- Unrealized holding losses trading securities (add to net income)

McGraw-Hill/Irwin © 2004 The McGraw-Hill Companies

Controlling Interests: Mergers and Acquisitions

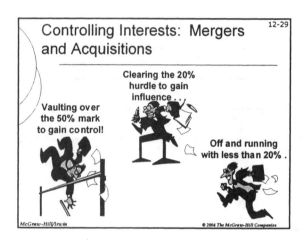

Vaulting over the 50% mark to gain control!

Clearing the 20% hurdle to gain influence . . .

Off and running with less than 20% .

McGraw-Hill/Irwin © 2004 The McGraw-Hill Companies

Controlling Interests: Mergers and Acquisitions

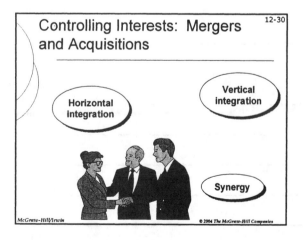

Horizontal integration

Vertical integration

Synergy

McGraw-Hill/Irwin © 2004 The McGraw-Hill Companies

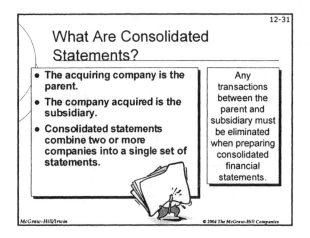

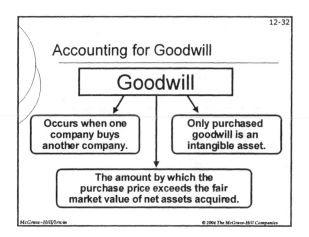

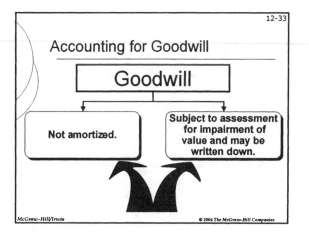

Consolidated Financial Statements

Dow Jones uses $100 million of its $368 million in current assets to purchase all the stock of IFNews for $100 million. IFNews' net assets (assets less liabilities) are $80 million at the date of purchase, but have a fair market value of $85 million.

Goodwill = ?
Goodwill = $100 million – $85 million = $15 million

Fair Value Adjustment = ?
Fair Value Adjustment = $85 million - $80 million
Fair Value Adjustment = $ 5 million

McGraw-Hill/Irwin   © 2004 The McGraw-Hill Companies

Consolidated Balance Sheet

	Dow Jones	IFN	Eliminations & Adjustments	Consolidated
ASSETS				
Current assets	$ 268			$ 268
Investment in IFN	100		$ (100)	-
Plant and property (net)	761	$ 30	5	796
Other assets	233	60		293
Goodwill			15	15
Total assets	$ 1,362	$ 90		$ 1,372
LIABILITIES & EQUITY				
Current liabilities	$ 587	$ 10		$ 597
Noncurrent liabilities	608			608
Stockholders' equity	167	80	(80)	167
Total liabilities & equity	$ 1,362	$ 90		$ 1,372

Eliminate the Investment against the Equity of IFN, establish goodwill, and record the assets at fair value.

McGraw-Hill/Irwin   © 2004 The McGraw-Hill Companies

Consolidated Income Statement

	Dow Jones	IFN	Adjustments	Consolidated
Revenues	$ 2,158	$ 120		$ 2,278
Expenses	(2,150)	(106)	(1)	(2,257)
Income	$ 8	$ 14	(1)	$ 21

$1 million additional depreciation on the $5 million additional fair value of assets acquired.

McGraw-Hill/Irwin   © 2004 The McGraw-Hill Companies

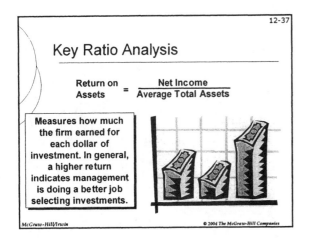

Chapter 13

Statement of Cash Flows

Business Background

Positive cash flows permit a company to . . .

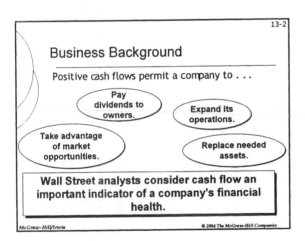

Pay dividends to owners.

Expand its operations.

Take advantage of market opportunities.

Replace needed assets.

Wall Street analysts consider cash flow an important indicator of a company's financial health.

Classifications on the Statement of Cash Flows

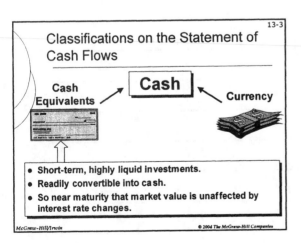

Cash Equivalents → **Cash** ← Currency

- Short-term, highly liquid investments.
- Readily convertible into cash.
- So near maturity that market value is unaffected by interest rate changes.

Classifications on the Statement of Cash Flows

13-4

The SCF must include the following three sections, as defined in *FASB Statement 95*:

❶ Operating Activities

❷ Investing Activities

❸ Financing Activities

McGraw-Hill/Irwin

© 2004 The McGraw-Hill Companies

THE BOSTON BEER COMPANY, INC.
CONSOLIDATED STATEMENT OF CASH FLOWS

13-5

(Unaudited)

In thousands for quarter ended	March 25, 2000
Cash flows from operating activities:	
Net income	$3,573
Adj. to reconcile net income to net cash provided by operating activities:	
Depreciation	1,408
Changes in assets and liabilities:	
Accounts receivable increase	(2,762)
Inventory increase	(220)
Prepaid expense decrease	1,549
Accounts payable decrease	(1,892)
Accrued expenses increase	1,266
Net cash provided by operating activities	2,922

Boston Beer uses the indirect method.

The indirect method is used by 98.3% of companies.

Statement continued . . . ◻◻◻

McGraw-Hill/Irwin

© 2004 The McGraw-Hill Companies

THE BOSTON BEER COMPANY, INC.
CONSOLIDATED STATEMENT OF CASH FLOWS

13-6

(Unaudited)

In thousands for quarter ended	March 25, 2000
Net cash provided by operating activities	$ 2,922
Cash flows for investing activities:	
Proceeds from sale of equipment	222
Purchases of equipment	(1,515)
Maturities (sale) of short-term investments	16,500
Purchase of short-term investments	(13,331)
Net cash provided by investing activities	1,876
Cash flows from financing activities:	
Purchase of treasury stock	(5,801)
Net proceeds from stock issuance	15
Net cash used in financing activities	(5,786)
Net increase (decrease) in cash & cash equivalents	(988)
Cash & cash equivalents at beginning of period	5,346
Cash & cash equivalents at end of period	$4,358

This ending cash balance should agree with the balance sheet.

McGraw-Hill/Irwin

© 2004 The McGraw-Hill Companies

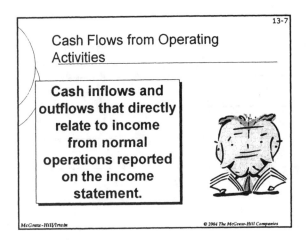

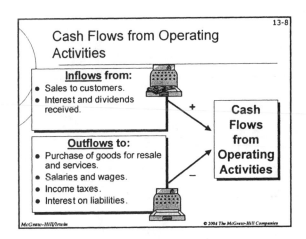

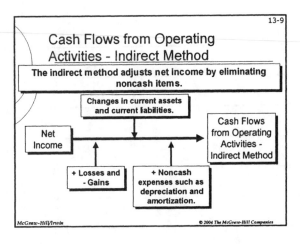

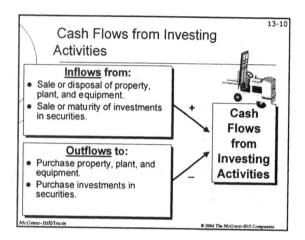

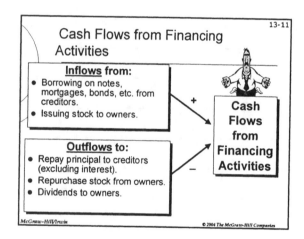

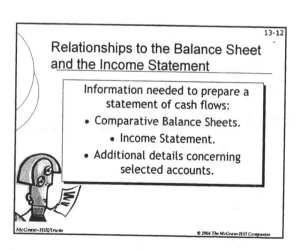

13-13

Relationships to the Balance Sheet and the Income Statement

$$\Delta \text{ Cash} = \Delta \text{ Liabilities} + \Delta \text{ Stockholders' Equity} - \Delta \text{ Noncash Assets}$$

Derives from . . .

Assets = Liabilities + Stockholders' Equity

McGraw-Hill/Irwin   © 2004 The McGraw-Hill Companies

13-14

Relationships to the Balance Sheet and the Income Statement

	Change in Account Balance During Year	
	Increase	**Decrease**
Current Assets	Subtract from net income.	Add to net income.
Current Liabilities	Add to net income.	Subtract from net income.

Use this table when adjusting Net Income to Operating Cash Flows using the indirect method.

McGraw-Hill/Irwin   © 2004 The McGraw-Hill Companies

13-15

Statement of Cash Flows Indirect Method Example

Use the following financial statements for The Boston Beer Company and prepare the Statement of Cash Flows for the quarter ended on March 25, 2000.

McGraw-Hill/Irwin   © 2004 The McGraw-Hill Companies

THE BOSTON BEER COMPANY, INC.
CONSOLIDATED BALANCE SHEET

(Unaudited) In Thousands	March 25, 2000	Dec. 25, 1999	Changes
ASSETS			
Current assets:			
Cash & cash equivalents	$ 4,358	$ 5,346	(988)
Short-term investments	35,830	38,999	(3,169)
Accounts Receivable	19,052	16,290	2,762
Inventories	15,876	15,656	220
Prepaid expenses	4,532	6,081	(1,549)
Total current assets	79,648	82,372	
Equipment, net	30,266	30,381	(115)
Total assets	$ 109,914	$ 112,753	

McGraw-Hill/Irwin © 2004 The McGraw-Hill Companies

THE BOSTON BEER COMPANY, INC.
CONSOLIDATED BALANCE SHEET

(Unaudited) In Thousands	March 25, 2000	Dec. 25, 1999	Changes
LIABILITIES & STOCKHOLDERS' EQUITY			
Current liabilities:			
Accounts payable	$ 14,414	$ 16,306	(1,892)
Accrued expenses	14,108	12,842	1,266
Total current liabilities	28,522	29,148	
Stockholders' Equity:			
Contributed capital	41,244	47,030	(5,786)
Retained earnings	40,148	36,575	3,573
Total stockholders' equity	81,392	83,605	
Total liabs & stockholders' equity	109,914	112,753	

McGraw-Hill/Irwin © 2004 The McGraw-Hill Companies

THE BOSTON BEER COMPANY, INC.
CONSOLIDATED STATEMENT OF INCOME
(Unaudited)

In Thousands Except Per Share Amounts	Quarter ended March 25, 2000
Sales	$49,276
Less excise taxes	5,019
Net Sales	44,257
Cost of sales	19,615
Gross profit	24,642
Operating expenses:	
Advertising, promotional, & selling expenses	16,140
General and administrative expenses	2,983
Total operating expenses	19,123
Operating income	5,519
Other income (expense):	
Interest income, net	514
Other income (expense), net	128
Total other income	642
Income before income taxes	6,161
Provision for income taxes	2,588
Net income	$3,573

The Statement of Cash Flows will begin with Boston Beer's Net Income from the Income Statement.

McGraw-Hill/Irwin © 2004 The McGraw-Hill Companies

THE BOSTON BEER COMPANY, INC.
CONSOLIDATED STATEMENT OF CASH FLOWS

(Unaudited)

In thousands for quarter ended	March 25, 2000
Cash flows from operating activities:	
Net income	$3,673

Next, adjust for the non-cash items included in net income.

For Boston Beer, the only non-cash adjustment is for depreciation expense ($1,408).

Since this number is not obvious in the Income Statement provided, it must be derived from other sources, such as the Notes to the Financial Statements or the General Ledger Trial Balance.

McGraw-Hill/Irwin   © 2004 The McGraw-Hill Companies

THE BOSTON BEER COMPANY, INC.
CONSOLIDATED STATEMENT OF CASH FLOWS

(Unaudited)

In thousands for quarter ended	March 25, 2000
Cash flows from operating activities:	
Net income	$3,673
Adj. to reconcile net income to net cash	
provided by operating activities:	
Depreciation	1,408

To complete the Cash flows from operating activities section, you must examine comparative balance sheets to determine the changes in current assets and current liabilities from the beginning of the period to the end of the period.

(Remember, we showed the balance sheets a few slides earlier.)

McGraw-Hill/Irwin   © 2004 The McGraw-Hill Companies

THE BOSTON BEER COMPANY, INC.
CONSOLIDATED STATEMENT OF CASH FLOWS

(Unaudited)

In thousands for quarter ended	March 25, 2000
Cash flows from operating activities:	
Net income	$3,673
Adj. to reconcile net income to net cash	
provided by operating activities:	
Depreciation	1,408
Changes in assets and liabilities:	
Accounts receivable increase	(2,762)
Inventory increase	(220)
Prepaid expense decrease	1,549
Accounts payable decrease	(1,892)
Accrued expenses increase	1,266
Net cash provided by operating activities	2,922

	Change in Account Balance During Year	
	Increase	Decrease
Current Assets	Subtract from net income.	Add to net income.
Current Liabilities	Add to net income.	Subtract from net income.

McGraw-Hill/I...   ...mpanies

THE BOSTON BEER COMPANY, INC.
CONSOLIDATED STATEMENT OF CASH FLOWS
(Unaudited)

13-22

In thousands for quarter ended	March 25, 2000
Net cash provided by operating activities	$ 2,922
Cash flows for investing activities:	
Proceeds from sale of equipment	222
Purchases of equipment	(1,515)
Maturities (sale) of short-term investments	16,500
Purchase of short-term investments	(13,331)
Net cash provided by investing activities	1,876
Cash flows from financing activities:	
Purchase of treasury stock	(5,801)
Net proceeds from stock issuance	15
Net cash used in financing activities	(5,786)
Net increase (decrease) in cash & cash equivalents	(988)
Cash & cash equivalents at beginning of period	5,346
Cash & cash equivalents at end of period	$4,358

Statement continued . . . ▯▯⬜➡

McGraw-Hill/Irwin   © 2004 The McGraw-Hill Companies

THE BOSTON BEER COMPANY, INC.
CONSOLIDATED STATEMENT OF CASH FLOWS
(Unaudited)

13-23

In thousands for quarter ended	March 25, 2000
Net cash provided by operating activities	$ 2,922
Cash flows for investing activities:	
Proceeds from sale of equipment	222
Purchases of equipment	(1,515)

The balance sheet indicates that Equipment decreased by $115 during the quarter.

If you had access to additional company information, you would discover that the company sold equipment with a book value of $222 and purchased $1,515 of new equipment. This is offset by $1,408 in depreciation expense (see the Cash Flows from Operating Activities).

McGraw-Hill/Irwin   © 2004 The McGraw-Hill Companies

THE BOSTON BEER COMPANY, INC.
CONSOLIDATED STATEMENT OF CASH FLOWS
(Unaudited)

13-24

In thousands for quarter ended	March 25, 2000
Net cash provided by operating activities	$ 2,922
Cash flows for investing activities:	
Proceeds from sale of equipment	222
Purchases of equipment	(1,515)
Maturities (sale) of short-term investments	16,500
Purchase of short-term investments	(13,331)
Net cash provided by investing activities	1,876

Short-term investments decreased by a net $3,169 during the quarter.

Further investigation of the accounting records reveals that Boston Beer sold short-term investments for $16,500 and purchased short-term investments for $13,331.

McGraw-Hill/Irwin   © 2004 The McGraw-Hill Companies

Slide 13-25

THE BOSTON BEER COMPANY, INC.
CONSOLIDATED STATEMENT OF CASH FLOWS

(Unaudited)

In thousands for quarter ended	March 25, 2000
Net cash provided by operating activities	$ 2,922
Cash flows for investing activities:	
Proceeds from sale of equipment	222
Purchases of equipment	(1,515)
Maturities (sale) of short-term investments	16,500
Purchase of short-term investments	(13,331)
Net cash provided by investing activities	1,876
Cash flows from financing activities:	
Purchase of treasury stock	(5,801)
Net proceeds from stock issuance	15
Net cash used in financing activities	(5,786)

Contributed Capital decreased by a net $5,786. Boston Beer repurchased $5,801 of outstanding stock, which is a cash outflow. The company also issued capital stock to employees for $15, which is a cash inflow.

Slide 13-26

THE BOSTON BEER COMPANY, INC.
CONSOLIDATED STATEMENT OF CASH FLOWS

(Unaudited)

In thousands for quarter ended	March 25, 2000
Net cash provided by operating activities	$ 2,922
Cash flows for investing activities:	
Proceeds from sale of equipment	222
Purchases of equipment	(1,515)
Maturities (sale) of short-term investments	16,500
Purchase of short-term investments	(13,331)
Net cash provided by investing activities	1,876
Cash flows from financing activities:	
Purchase of treasury stock	(5,801)
Net proceeds from stock issuance	15
Net cash used in financing activities	(5,786)
Net increase (decrease) in cash & cash equivalents	(988)
Cash & cash equivalents at beginning of period	5,346
Cash & cash equivalents at end of period	$4,358

Now we can reconcile the change in cash to the ending cash balance that appears on the Balance Sheet.

Slide 13-27

THE BOSTON BEER COMPANY, INC.
CONSOLIDATED STATEMENT OF CASH FLOWS

(Unaudited)

In thousands for quarter ended	March 25, 2000
Net cash provided by operating activities	$ 2,922
Cash flows for investing activities:	

Required Supplemental Information:

1. Cash paid for taxes and interest.

2. Significant non-cash investing and financing activities.

Net cash used in financing activities	(5,786)
Net increase (decrease) in cash & cash equivalents	(988)
Cash & cash equivalents at beginning of period	5,346
Cash & cash equivalents at end of period	$4,358

A Comparison of the Direct and Indirect Methods

- Net cash flow is the same for both methods.
- The direct method provides more detail about cash from operating activities.
- The investing and financing sections for the two methods are identical.

McGraw-Hill/Irwin   © 2004 The McGraw-Hill Companies

Direct Method Operating Activities

THE BOSTON BEER COMPANY, INC.
CONSOLIDATED STATEMENT OF CASH FLOWS
(Unaudited)

In thousands for quarter ended	March 26, 2000
Cash flows from operating activities:	
Cash collected from customers	$41,495
Cash collected for interest	553
Cash payments to suppliers	(21,727)
Cash payments for expenses	(14,811)
Cash payments for income taxes	(2,588)
Net cash provided by operating activities	$ 2,922

Remember that when we prepared the operating section using the indirect method, we also arrived at net cash inflow of $2,922.

McGraw-Hill/Irwin   © 2004 The McGraw-Hill Companies

End of Chapter 13

Chester, ol' buddy, I wonder if you could help me with a little cash flow problem I'm having?

McGraw-Hill/Irwin   © 2004 The McGraw-Hill Companies

14-1

Chapter 14

Analyzing Financial Statements

14-2

Understanding The Business

FINANCIAL STATEMENT USERS

MANAGEMENT	EXTERNAL DECISION MAKERS
⇩	⇩
. . . uses accounting data to make product pricing and expansion decisions.	. . . use accounting data for investment, credit, tax, and public policy decisions.

McGraw-Hill/Irwin © 2004 The McGraw-Hill Companies

14-3

Understanding The Business

THREE TYPES OF FINANCIAL STATEMENT INFORMATION

Past Performance	Present Condition	Future Performance
Income, sales volume, cash flows, return-on-investments, EPS.	Assets, debt, inventory, various ratios.	Sales and earnings trends are good indicators of future performance.

McGraw-Hill/Irwin © 2004 The McGraw-Hill Companies

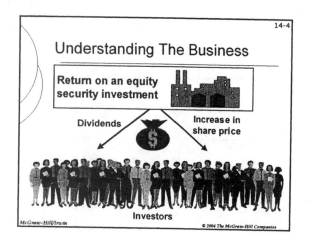

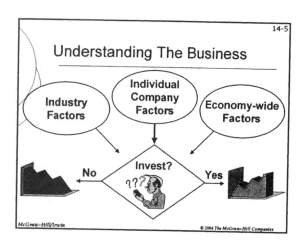

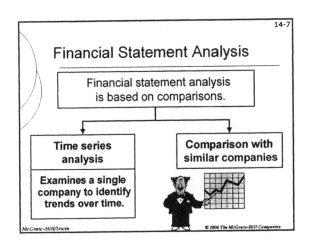

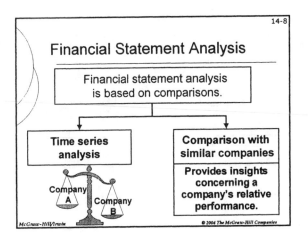

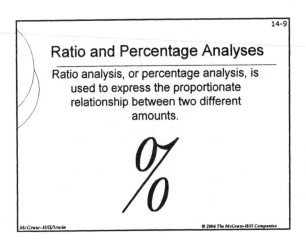

Component Percentages

Express each item on a particular statement as a percentage of a single base amount.

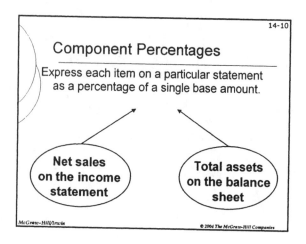

Net sales on the income statement

Total assets on the balance sheet

Component Percentages Example

The comparative income statements of Home Depot 2001 and 2000 appear on the next slide.

Prepare component percentage income statements where net sales equal 100%.

Home Depot

Component Percentages

HOME DEPOT
Comparative Income Statements (Condensed)
Amounts in Millions Except Per Share Data

	2001	Percent	2000	Percent
Net Sales	$ 45,738	100.0%	$ 38,434	100.0%
Cost of merchandise sold	32,057		27,023	
Gross profit	13,681		11,411	
Operating expenses	9,490		7,603	
Operating Income	4,191		3,808	
Interest and Investment Income	47		37	
Interest Expense	21		41	
Earnings Before Income Taxes	4,217		3,804	
Income Taxes	1,636		1,484	
Net Earnings	$ 2,581		$ 2,320	
Basic Earnings Per Share	$ 1.11		$ 1.03	
Weighted-Average Number of Common Shares Outstanding	2,315		2,244	
Diluted Earnings Per Share	$ 1.10		$ 1.00	

Component Percentages

HOME DEPOT
Comparative Income Statements (Condensed)
Amounts in Millions Except Per Share Data

	2001	Percent	2000	Percent
Net Sales	$ 45,738	100.0%	$ 38,434	100.0%
Cost of merchandise sold	32,057	70.1%	27,023	
Gross profit	13,681		11,411	
Operating expenses	9,490		7,603	
Operating Income	4,191		3,808	
Interest and Investment Income				
Interest Expense				
Earnings Before Income Taxes				
Income Taxes				
Net Earnings	$ 2,581		$ 2,320	
Basic Earnings Per Share	$ 1.11		$ 1.03	
Weighted-Average Number of				
Common Shares Outstanding	2,315		2,244	
Diluted Earnings Per Share	$ 1.10		$ 1.00	

2001 Cost ÷ 2001 Sales

McGraw-Hill/Irwin   © 2004 The McGraw-Hill Companies

Component Percentages

HOME DEPOT
Comparative Income Statements (Condensed)
Amounts in Millions Except Per Share Data

	2001	Percent	2000	Percent
Net Sales	$ 45,738	100.0%	$ 38,434	100.0%
Cost of merchandise sold	32,057	70.1%	27,023	70.3%
Gross profit	13,681	29.9%	11,411	29.7%
Operating expenses	9,490	20.7%	7,603	19.8%
Operating Income	4,191	9.2%	3,808	9.9%
Interest and Investment Income	47	0.1%	37	0.1%
Interest Expense	21	0.0%	41	0.1%
Earnings Before Income Taxes	4,217	9.2%	3,804	9.9%
Income Taxes	1,636	3.6%	1,484	3.9%
Net Earnings	$ 2,581	5.6%	$ 2,320	6.0%
Basic Earnings Per Share	$ 1.11		$ 1.03	
Weighted-Average Number of				
Common Shares Outstanding	2,315		2,244	
Diluted Earnings Per Share	$ 1.10		$ 1.00	

McGraw-Hill/Irwin   © 2004 The McGraw-Hill Companies

Now, let's look at some commonly used ratios.

McGraw-Hill/Irwin   © 2004 The McGraw-Hill Companies

Commonly Used Ratios

The 2001 and 2000 balance sheets for Home Depot are presented next.

We will be referring to these financial statements throughout the ratio analyses.

Home Depot

McGraw-Hill/Irwin   © 2004 The McGraw-Hill Companies

Comparative Statements

HOME DEPOT
Comparative Balance Sheets (Condensed)
Amounts in Millions

Assets	2001	2000
Cash and Cash Equivalents	$ 167	$ 168
Receivables, net	835	587
Merchandise inventories	6,556	5,489
Other Current Assets	219	146
Total Current Assets	7,777	6,390
Property and Equipment, at cost	15,232	11,890
Less Accumulated Depreciation	2,164	1,663
Net Property and Equipment	13,068	10,227
Other Assets	540	464
Total Assets	$ 21,385	$ 17,081

Continued

McGraw-Hill/Irwin   © 2004 The McGraw-Hill Companies

Comparative Statements

HOME DEPOT
Comparative Balance Sheets (Condensed)
Amounts in Millions

Liabilities	2001	2000
Current Liabilities	$ 4,385	$ 3,656
Noncurrent Liabilities	1,996	1,084
Total Liabilities	6,381	4,740
Stockholders' Equity		
Common Stock, $.05 par	116	115
Paid-in Capital	4,810	4,319
Retained Earnings	10,151	7,941
Accumulated Other Comprehensive Income	(67)	(27)
Total	15,010	12,348
Less: Treasury Stock	6	7
Total Stockholders' Equity	15,004	12,341
Total Liabilities & Stockholders' Equity	$ 21,385	$ 17,081

McGraw-Hill/Irwin   © 2004 The McGraw-Hill Companies

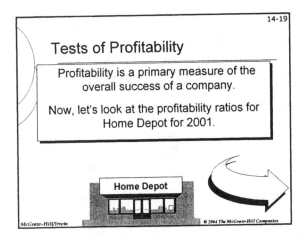

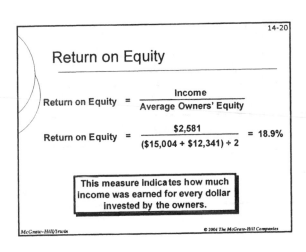

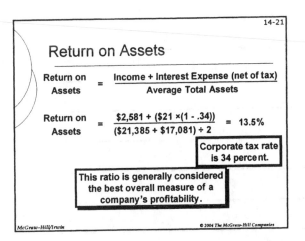

Financial Leverage

$$\text{Financial Leverage} = \text{Return on Equity} - \text{Return on Assets}$$

$$5.4\% = 18.9\% - 13.5\%$$

> **Financial leverage is the advantage or disadvantage that occurs as the result of earning a return on equity that is different from the return on assets.**

McGraw-Hill/Irwin   © 2004 The McGraw-Hill Companies

Earnings per Share (EPS)

$$\text{EPS} = \frac{\text{Income}}{\text{Average Number of Shares of Common Stock Outstanding}}$$

$$\text{EPS} = \frac{\$2,581}{(2,324 + 2,304) \div 2} = \$1.12$$

> **Earnings per share is probably the single most widely watched financial ratio.**

McGraw-Hill/Irwin   © 2004 The McGraw-Hill Companies

Quality of Income

$$\text{Quality of Income} = \frac{\text{Cash Flow from Operating Activities}}{\text{Net Income}}$$

Cash Flow from Operating Activities		
Net Income		$ 2,581
Add:	Depreciation and Amortization	601
	Increase in Current Liabilities	754
	Increase in Income Taxes Payable	151
	Other	30
Deduct:	Increase in Receivables, net	(246)
	Increase in Merchandise Inventories	(1,075)
Cash Flow from Operating Activities		$ 2,796

McGraw-Hill/Irwin   © 2004 The McGraw-Hill Companies

Quality of Income

$$\text{Quality of Income} = \frac{\text{Cash Flow from Operating Activities}}{\text{Net Income}}$$

$$\text{Quality of Income} = \frac{\$2,796}{\$2,581} = 1.08$$

A ratio higher than 1 indicates higher-quality earnings.

McGraw-Hill/Irwin
© 2004 The McGraw-Hill Companies

Profit Margin

$$\text{Profit Margin} = \frac{\text{Income (before Extraordinary Items)}}{\text{Net Sales}}$$

$$\text{Profit Margin} = \frac{\$2,581}{\$45,738} = 5.6\%$$

This ratio describes a company's ability to earn income from sales.

McGraw-Hill/Irwin
© 2004 The McGraw-Hill Companies

Fixed Asset Turnover

$$\text{Fixed Asset Turnover} = \frac{\text{Net Sales Revenue}}{\text{Average Net Fixed Assets}}$$

$$\text{Fixed Asset Turnover} = \frac{\$45,738}{(\$13,068 + \$10,227) \div 2} = 3.9$$

This ratio measures a company's ability to generate sales given an investment in fixed assets.

McGraw-Hill/Irwin
© 2004 The McGraw-Hill Companies

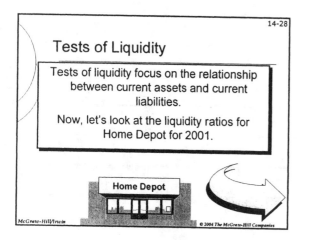

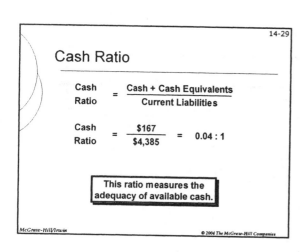

Current Ratio

$$\text{Current Ratio} = \frac{\text{Current Assets}}{\text{Current Liabilities}}$$

$$\text{Current Ratio} = \frac{\$7,777}{\$4,385} = 1.77 : 1$$

This ratio measures the ability of the company to pay current debts as they become due.

McGraw-Hill/Irwin   © 2004 The McGraw-Hill Companies

Quick Ratio (Acid Test)

$$\frac{\text{Quick}}{\text{Ratio}} = \frac{\text{Quick Assets}}{\text{Current Liabilities}}$$

$$\frac{\text{Quick}}{\text{Ratio}} = \frac{\$1,012}{\$4,385} = .23 : 1$$

Cash & Cash Equivalents	$ 167
Receivables, net	835
Short-term Investments	10
Quick Assets	$ 1,012

This ratio is like the current ratio but measures the company's immediate ability to pay debts.

McGraw-Hill/Irwin   © 2004 The McGraw-Hill Companies

Receivable Turnover

$$\frac{\text{Receivable}}{\text{Turnover}} = \frac{\text{Net Credit Sales}}{\text{Average Net Trade Receivables}}$$

$$\frac{\text{Receivable}}{\text{Turnover}} = \frac{\$45,738}{(\$835 + \$587) \div 2} = 64 \text{ times}$$

This ratio measures how quickly a company collects its accounts receivable.

McGraw-Hill/Irwin   © 2004 The McGraw-Hill Companies

Average Age of Receivables

$$\frac{\text{Average Age}}{\text{of Receivables}} = \frac{\text{Days in Year}}{\text{Receivable Turnover}}$$

$$\frac{\text{Average Age}}{\text{of Receivables}} = \frac{365}{64} = 5.7 \text{ days}$$

This ratio measures the average number of days it takes to collect receivables.

McGraw-Hill/Irwin   © 2004 The McGraw-Hill Companies

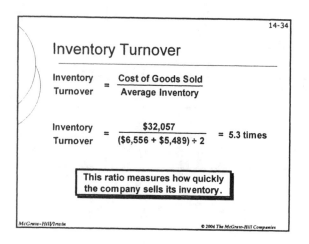

Inventory Turnover

$$\frac{\text{Inventory}}{\text{Turnover}} = \frac{\text{Cost of Goods Sold}}{\text{Average Inventory}}$$

$$\frac{\text{Inventory}}{\text{Turnover}} = \frac{\$32,057}{(\$6,556 + \$5,489) \div 2} = 5.3 \text{ times}$$

This ratio measures how quickly the company sells its inventory.

McGraw-Hill/Irwin   © 2004 The McGraw-Hill Companies

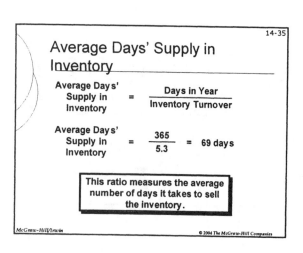

Average Days' Supply in Inventory

$$\frac{\text{Average Days'}}{\text{Supply in}}_{\text{Inventory}} = \frac{\text{Days in Year}}{\text{Inventory Turnover}}$$

$$\frac{\text{Average Days'}}{\text{Supply in}}_{\text{Inventory}} = \frac{365}{5.3} = 69 \text{ days}$$

This ratio measures the average number of days it takes to sell the inventory.

McGraw-Hill/Irwin   © 2004 The McGraw-Hill Companies

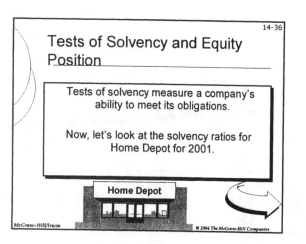

Tests of Solvency and Equity Position

Tests of solvency measure a company's ability to meet its obligations.

Now, let's look at the solvency ratios for Home Depot for 2001.

Home Depot

McGraw-Hill/Irwin   © 2004 The McGraw-Hill Companies

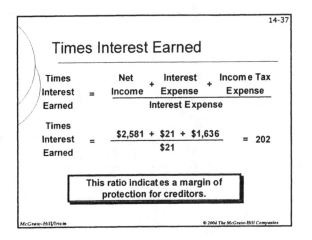

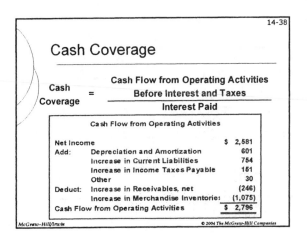

Cash Coverage

$$\text{Cash Coverage} = \frac{\text{Cash Flow from Operating Activities Before Interest and Taxes}}{\text{Interest Paid}}$$

$$\text{Cash Coverage} = \frac{\$2,796 + \$16 + \$1,386}{\$16} = 262$$

Cash payments made for:	
Interest	$ 16
Income Taxes	1,386

This ratio compares the cash generated with the cash obligations of the period.

McGraw-Hill/Irwin © 2004 The McGraw-Hill Companies

Debt/Equity Ratio

$$\text{Debt/Equity Ratio} = \frac{\text{Total Liabilities}}{\text{Owners' Equity}}$$

$$\text{Debt/Equity Ratio} = \frac{\$6,381}{\$15,004} = 0.43$$

This ratio measures the amount of liabilities that exists for each $1 invested by the owners.

McGraw-Hill/Irwin   © 2004 The McGraw-Hill Companies

Market Tests

Market tests relate the current market price of a share of stock to an indicator of the return that might accrue to the investor.

Now, let's look at the market tests for Home Depot for 2001.

McGraw-Hill/Irwin   © 2004 The McGraw-Hill Companies

Price/Earnings (P/E) Ratio

$$\text{P/E Ratio} = \frac{\text{Current Market Price Per Share}}{\text{Earnings Per Share}}$$

$$\text{P/E Ratio} = \frac{\$35}{\$1.12} = 31.3$$

A recent price for Home Depot stock was $35 per share.

This ratio measures the relationship between the current market price of the stock and its earnings per share.

McGraw-Hill/Irwin   © 2004 The McGraw-Hill Companies

Dividend Yield Ratio

$$\frac{\text{Dividend}}{\text{Yield}} = \frac{\text{Dividends Per Share}}{\text{Market Price Per Share}}$$

$$\frac{\text{Dividend}}{\text{Yield}} = \frac{\$0.16}{\$35} = 0.46\%$$

Home Depot paid dividends of $.16 per share when the market price was $35 per share.

This ratio is often used to compare the dividend-paying performance of different investment alternatives.

McGraw-Hill/Irwin   © 2004 The McGraw-Hill Companies

Other Analytical Considerations

In addition to financial ratios, special factors might affect company analysis:

- Rapid growth.
- Uneconomical expansion.
- Subjective factors.

McGraw-Hill/Irwin   © 2004 The McGraw-Hill Companies

Interpreting Ratios

Ratios may be interpreted by comparison with ratios of other companies or with industry average ratios.

Ratios may vary because of the company's industry characteristics, nature of operations, size, and accounting policies.

McGraw-Hill/Irwin   © 2004 The McGraw-Hill Companies

Efficient Markets

A securities market in which prices fully reflect available information is called an efficient market.

In an efficient market, a company's stock reacts quickly when new, relevant information is released about the company.

Late Breaking News

McGraw-Hill/Irwin © 2004 The McGraw-Hill Companies

End of Chapter 14

McGraw-Hill/Irwin © 2004 The McGraw-Hill Companies